The Unspoken Truth

New
Century
Books

The Unspoken Truth

Race, Culture and Other Taboos

Frank Borzellieri

New Century Foundation

Copyright 1999 by New Century Foundation

All rights reserved

First Printing

New Century Books
Box 527
Oakton, Virginia 22124-0527

Tel. (703) 716-0900
Fax. (703) 716-0932

www.amren.com

ISBN 0-9656383-1-6
Library of Congress Catalog Card Number: 98-067775

Cover design by Rodney Jung

Manufactured in the United States of America

Dedicated

To My Parents

Acknowledgments

Thanks, Thanks a Lot, and Special Thanks

Whether on the acknowledgment page of a book or at the Academy Awards, people are reluctant to list acknowledgments for fear of leaving someone out or not giving people their proper due. If such a tragic lapse should befall me and I forget someone, may I be forced to lobby for multicultural and bilingual education. The people I acknowledge here all had their unique influence on me and on this book. Some helped in research, others in ideas for articles, still others for encouragement and support. Not everyone listed is in agreement with all or even most of my views and many judged my essays with a critical eye and offered alternative views (which succeeded to varying degrees.) The important thing is that the impact of all these people was positive.

So thanks to:

George Anastasiou, Thomas Ballou, Lorraine Barra, Art Beroff, Robert Blumetti, Peter Brimelow, Thomas Brock, Steve Brown, Patrick Buchanan, John Ciampoli, Terez Czapp, Gus Dallas, John DeLoca, Jay Diamond, Maria Doherty, Louise Emanuel, Samuel Francis, Robert Gennaro, Jean Giunta, Bob Grant, John Haggerty, Tanya Handler, Michael Hart, Chuck Heston, William Iapalucci, Roy Innis, Rodney Jung, Joseph Kasper, Melinda Katz (Meow!), Rose Kim, Catherine Knett, Kurt Kraska, Alice Lemos, Michael Levin, Jerold Levine, Rosemarie Limbacher, Herbert London, James Lubinskas, Wayne Lutton, Peter Mannarino, Dorinda Mittiga, Helen Morris, Ernest Naspretto, Linda Ocasio, Theodore O'Keefe, Elaine Perri, Melissa Phillips, Christine Piacente, Michelle Pinto, Anthony Pranzo, Jerry Preiser, William Ramsey, Bruno Sammartino, Jules Santagata, Rabbi Mayer Schiller, Jeff Simmons, Ben Shoer, Father James Thornton, John Toscano, A.R. Trasque, Robert Unger, Josephine Venticinque.

Special Thanks

Also, thanks to the man who wrote the Forward to this book, Jared Taylor, and his entire staff at American Renaissance Publications. So much of the work in this book is the result of exhaustive research done by and with the help of Jared and American Renaissance. If Jared had not already done the research, he often pointed me in the right (literally) direction. I'm grateful for his ideological kinship and for his friendship. As Ed Norton would say, he's one of nature's noblemen.

Special thanks to Walter Sanchez, my editor at the Ledger-Observer Newspaper group, which publishes my weekly column. The great ones often don't realize their special qualities, and Walter, a political moderate, is a genuine believer in the First Amendment and the right of people to express their views, not just a pretender to the idea. When he began running my column, he was inundated with calls of objection from small-time politicians and hysterical liberals who heaped scorn on his decision. To his great credit, he basically told them where to get off. Although Walter never complained at the time, it must have been unnerving and exasperating for a civilized man to be confronted with such a level of irrationality and paranoia by fanatical misfits who cannot tolerate an alternative point of view. Walter Sanchez, in his own way, has done James Madison proud.

And finally, thanks to my agent, Richard Valcourt, for his sound advice and input, and to the New Century Foundation for all the work they put into publishing this book.

Contents

FORWARD	1
INTRODUCTION	5
1. CULTURE	9
Race and the Right of Free Speech	11
Are All Cultures Equal?	13
Diversity is Our Weakness	15
Wither Washington?	18
Are All Men Created Equal?	20
Animal Rights Terrorists	22
The Myth of Integration	25
From Charity to Welfare	27
Beware of Earth Day	29
Multicultural Madness	32
What is Racism?	34
Those Pesky North Asians	37
Why Race Hoaxes Are Common	39

	Pledging Allegiance to Whom?	42
	The Invented Indian	44
	In Defense of Militias	47
	Curing What Ails Khalid Muhammad	50
2.	**AFFIRMATIVE ACTION**	53
	The Real "Discrimination"	55
	Laws of Lunacy	57
	"Disparate Impact" and Race-norming	59
	That Elusive Test Bias	62
3.	**IMMIGRATION**	65
	Damn Lies and Immigration Myths	67
	Immigration: Social Calamity	69
	Alien Nation	71
	Last Gasp of White America?	74
4.	**POLITICS AND GOVERNMENT**	77
	Bogus Charges of Bank Bigotry	79
	Reparations Madness	81
	The National Endowment for Pornography	86

Statehood for Puerto Rico?	89
A "Sorry" Excuse for a President	91
UN, Get Lost Already	94
The Road to World Government	96
Impeach Him for Treason, Not Sex	99
5. CRIME AND GUN CONTROL	**103**
The Unjust Saga of Bernhard Goetz	105
Getting Away With Perjury	118
Freedom and the Brady Law	120
The Color of Crime	123
Race and the Death Penalty	125
Gun Locks: The New Chic Craze	128
6. EDUCATION	**131**
The Bilingual Follies	133
School Desegregation: Judicial Tyranny	135
Abolish Public Education	137
The Sex Education Racket	141

7. **PROFILES** 157

    The Man of the Millennium (Columbus) 159

    Goldwater: The Original Extremist 161

    Meow! Katz For Congress (Melinda Katz) 164

    Bruno: Still the Living Legend (Sammartino) 166

    Holy Moses! (Charlton Heston) 168

    The Liberals' Problem With Lincoln 171

    Michael Levin's Last Laugh 173

    The King Has No Clothes (Martin Luther King) 175

8. **BOOK REVIEWS** 185

    White, Black, A Liberal Hack 187

    What "Mainstream" Blacks Think 193

    Heard It Through the Grapevine 195

ABOUT THE AUTHOR 199

Forward

by Jared Taylor

The columns that Frank Borzellieri writes for the *Ledger-Observer* newspapers and other publications -- and the reactions he gets -- remind me of one of Mark Twain's remarks: "Nothing astonishes people more than to tell them the truth." Witty old cynic that he was, Twain wasn't writing about how we reply when a lady asks if we like her latest hairdo. He was thinking of the secret truths that all societies shield from view with taboos, myths, and what we today call political correctness.

Twain did not have political correctness to deal with, and it's a pity he didn't; it wouldn't have survived the hilarious blasts he would have unleashed against it. But he did have silly posturings to ridicule, windbags to deflate, and lies to expose -- and he knew that every age would have its posturings, windbags, and lies. I do not doubt that Twain now smiles down on those who battle these scourges, and that he directs a particularly encouraging smile in the direction of Frank Borzellieri.

The reason, of course, is that Frank Borzellieri and untruth are incompatible, and that when he sees the nonsense that passes for today's political wisdom he cannot sit idly by. He rolls up his sleeves, spits on his hands, and -- well -- astonishes people. There has never been another time in the history of America when even small doses of truth caused such astonishment, and Frank doesn't stop with small doses.

Mark Twain didn't say this, but when you make it your business to astonish people by telling them the truth, they don't always react with relief and gratitude. People become very attached to their illusions and don't enjoy seeing them punctured. What makes the business of astonishment-through-truth so important today is the desperation and even viciousness with which the defenders of orthodoxy fight to protect their illusions. Debates that should be about simple, verifiable facts are often turned into professions of faith and denunciations of evil. It is almost impossible to debate a liberal without discovering something that is half-mania, half-religion. Indeed, one of liberalism's most unattractive traits is its tone of moral superiority, its insistence that dissenters are not merely wrong but heretical.

I was once on a radio program with a host who declared that she was "a bleeding heart liberal and damn proud of it." Why, I asked, was she *proud* of her politics. When she hesitated, I asked if it was because being a liberal meant she could feel morally superior to people like me. She conceded that it was. How strange are the ways of liberals! Can we ever trust the motives of someone who chooses his politics, at least in part, because they come with a little shiver of moral superiority? And is not the record of liberalism the sad legacy of trying to do good by *feeling* good?

But now that public policy has become an opportunity to exhibit politically correct virtues, people like Frank Borzellieri who stand for truth, fairness, and common sense become targets of invective and excommunication. Racist, Nazi, homophobe, bigot -- he has been called all these names and more. When the other side doesn't like his facts, it stoops to name-calling. It would be hard to think of a more graceless way for opponents to admit they have lost the argument, but they don't seem to realize how hysterical it makes them sound. These are the people who, a few centuries ago, burned dissenters at the stake.

But there is something else that the readers of this volume should know about Frank Borzellieri. He doesn't just talk and write about how things ought to be. He makes them happen. He has won far more notoriety as an elected school board member and candidate for public office than as a columnist.

Some people go into politics to *be* something. They think political power will make them respected and happy, and for them politics is about winning elections -- not about principles, convictions, or vision. Our country is full of people like that. Fortunately, there are a few men who go into politics to *do* something. Principles, convictions, and vision are what they are about. For them, elected office is not an end in itself but a way to build America, to fix what is wrong and improve what is right. They proclaim in public what they think in private, they are faithful to their principles, and they do not trim their views to suit their audiences.

Such men are an anachronism in this era of political consultants and perpetual poll-taking. George Washington and Thomas Jefferson didn't need consultants to tell them what to think or say; they would have been appalled by the idea. Frank Borzellieri doesn't need consultants either. As this collection shows, he knows very well what to think, and would laugh at the idea of changing his views to win a few more votes. What's right is right no matter how astonishing and no matter how much others may resist it.

Of course, millions of Americans know very well that Frank Borzellieri is right, that he says in print what others know in their bones but are afraid to say. But why bother? Why take the heat? Why endure the insults of the people who have a near-monopoly on public discourse? For only one reason: *Frank Borzellieri cares passionately about the future of America.* Unlike talk show hosts or editorial writers who choose their politics for reasons of vanity, Frank's greatest concern is to restore America's greatness.

Today we are stumbling badly, as elite opinion turns away from the wisdom of the men who founded and built America. But with just a few more men like Frank Borzellieri we can turn this country back towards their wisdom, back towards the sturdy qualities of honesty, self-reliance, integrity, and patriotism that inspired the men of our past and made them great. So long as there are men of courage, of vision, and of principle, who are prepared not only to speak their minds but to lead their communities and their nation, we can regain what we have lost and relaunch that task to which our ancestors pledged their lives, their fortunes and their sacred honor.

Introduction

In many ways, it is much more difficult to construct a book that is a collection of essays than one that is a straight narrative. For one thing, it takes an inordinate amount of time for a collection of writings to accumulate. Then, there is the business of selecting those writings which most complement each other in a collection which, by definition, is comprised of topics that are somewhat different from each other. Those differences, however, are narrower in this case, since almost all of my essays here relate to culture and politics.

I have tried over the years to distinguish my writings by a certain style, depth of research and persuasive analyses and conclusions which hopefully make for enlightening and worthwhile reading. In addition, I have always endeavored to make my columns forever topical by writing pieces as official statements on substantive issues as often as possible. Circumstances in American society change, but bedrock principles do not. In that sense, it may be easier to put together a collection of essays for me than for most other writers. I believe (and hope) the writings compiled in this book can be used as a sort of reference tool on issues that are rarely, if ever, addressed from the point of view that I take.

As this is being written, my literary agent is searching for a publisher for my second book, which is a narrative of my unique political travails. Not only is that the easier book to write, but it is written in the first person, as it is telling my own story. The essays in this book, conversely, are almost all written omnisciently, from the third person. This is merely a matter of style, the one I usually utilize. Many columnists write from the first person, but I wanted the focus on issues, analysis and conclusions, not on myself.

The first article I had published by a major publication was shortly after graduation from college when *Newsday* printed my opinion piece on its op-ed page supporting the re-election of Ronald Reagan. Soon after, *USA Today* magazine published my longer essay on gun control. It was during those times that I realized I was too opinionated to write straight news as a reporter and would stick to editorial writing.

Every essay herein was once published and read somewhere else, so there have already been reactions to them in one form or another. Most of this collection deals with the subject of race. There is a very important reason for that. It is the same reason that most of my essays at the time they were originally published dealt with race. There is, quite honestly, a hunger for the topic which few others will touch — the true third rail of American political and cultural life.

Certainly, there are many fine conservative columnists who take the correct positions on affirmative action, for example, or immigration. But the raw bluntness which the issue of race requires is extremely rare outside of journals of opinion which deal specifically with race. At first, many of my columns on race were shocking to many people. But they were shocking *even to people who agreed with me.* These people were shocked that such straightforward commentary on race even saw the light of day. In private conversations on race through the years, when I would make a politically incorrect observation, I would invariably be met with the response, "Yeah, but you can't say that."

Oh, yes you can.

Moreover, since my views have become public, I am constantly met with the opinion that I am merely saying out loud what most people say in the privacy of their living rooms. But the only thing that should really matter in responsible writing is not whether everyone agrees, but whether my essays are well-researched, carefully thought out and motivated by the desire to tell the truth, even if some think it should be the *unspoken* truth.

My friend Samuel Francis, the beleaguered columnist, was fired by the *Washington Times* for writing an article on race deemed unacceptable. Other careers have been threatened and short-circuited because of politically incorrect views on race. This is especially disheartening when people like Sam's detractors won't even bother to refute his words, but merely seek to discredit his character and attach sinister motives to him.

As a conservative and an elected member of a New York City school board, and as someone who has held various titles in organizations of different ideological imperatives, I have always been first and foremost a journalist and writer. It is only in recent years that I have seen fit to concentrate more on race than on other issues. Believe me, when there is more honest public commentary about race, I will write about it a lot less.

Certainly, America's problems are impacted by many factors: the decline of morality, the absence of God in schools, confiscatory taxation, tyrannical gun control, rampant street crime and a myriad of social ills that were not adversely affecting America as recently as a generation ago.

The essays put together here are as unfettered from political niceties as humanly possible. I refuse to succumb to any temptation to "tone it down" just to be seen as more acceptable. As long as my work is well-researched and cogently presented, there should be nothing to worry about. It may be hopeless, but if liberals would just try to have an open mind — and not try to decipher my motives (which are pure, I assure them) — they may actually see some merit in the conclusions drawn here. If such a liberal newspaper as *Newsday* can be fair enough to print something with which they disagree, my detractors should be able to be tolerant enough to read the views expressed here without screaming.

I think it is only human nature to react to a column and write a responding letter more so when you dislike it than when you agree with it. The reactions to some of my essays have been vociferous to say the least. I cannot honestly say this makes me unhappy. Receiving negative letters has always given me the feeling that I'm probably making some sense.

Finally, being a prolific writer has given me the opportunity to reveal to my public some personal favorite people and interests of mine, like the profiles on wrestling legend Bruno Sammartino and actor Charlton Heston and my occasional references to baseball and *The Honeymooners*. It has also given me the chance to have some fun, as with my column on adorable Democratic legislator Melinda Katz. After all, if I couldn't have fun and if I took myself and these issue too seriously all the time, I wouldn't be able to keep that sharp edge that drives the liberals crazy. *Ridgewood, NY December1, 1998*

1
CULTURE

Race and the Right of Free Speech

Race is America's eternal cross. It is the most dishonestly discussed topic in American society. Race — not social security — is the true third rail of American politics. Touch it, and your career could be threatened, your opinions stifled, and your basic right to free speech obliterated. Race is the one issue that makes grown people tremble.

There is no issue in American society on which public statements differ so much from private opinions. Liberals may deplore this, but deep down, no one can deny it. Race is the greatest problem and the source of the greatest conflict in America today. Yet, there is no honest discussion. This is the great American ironic tragedy. It is precisely on our most profound problem that we need the most frank discussion. But political correctness and the orthodoxies of our time virtually forbid it. Since any frank discussion of race paralyzes the intellectual elite in America, and results in ad hominem attacks of bigotry on those who initiate it, we see virtually none of it. Those who challenge racial orthodoxy do so at their own risk. Few, therefore, choose to do so.

Peter Brimelow, a British immigrant and senior editor of *Forbes* magazine, has written, "As an immigrant, I was fascinated... to watch the mere threat of an accusation of racism send the native-born Americans scattering for cover like hightailing rabbits."

It is virtually impossible to have a rational discussion on the subject of race, so driven by emotion and fanaticism are today's thought police, so much so that they cannot and will not tolerate an alternative opinion. Rather than discuss civilly, the defenders of the faith engage in endless motive-seeking. But when the witch hunt finally ends, an argument must ultimately stand or fall on the facts. Oh yes, the facts.

Endless "solutions" regarding the race problem — government welfare programs, civil rights laws, special commissions, minority set-asides, national discussions, sensitivity training, anti-bias laws, race-norming, forced integration, school busing and, of course, affirmative action — have all failed miserably. They have failed because the problem was not addressed honestly. Just as 20,000 gun control laws have not curbed gun crimes because such laws misguidedly focus on depriving the honest citizen rather than the criminal, so do these endless race solutions add up to nothing more than smoke and mirrors.

For example, 130 years after slavery ended, forty years after Brown vs. Board of Education, and more than thirty years after the civil rights laws of the 1960's, black Americans continue to live at the margins of society despite everything that has been tried. These solutions all failed and will continue to fail because the basic premise on which they are based is false. And that basic premise is that race doesn't matter, there are really no meaningful racial differences, and white racism is to blame for all of society's racial problems.

Of course, if the races were interchangeable, then race would be nothing more than a biological curiosity. It is because race matters so much that practically all decisions people make are based — directly or indirectly — on considerations of race.

Problems which appear on the surface to have nothing to do with race — crime, housing, welfare, property values — need only be examined slightly *beneath the surface* to see that race is the central factor. The racial composition of a city will reveal as much about its crime situation as the city's law enforcement policies. Likewise, race governs almost every decision people make in their personal lives — where they buy a home, where they work, where they send their children to school, who they marry, what clubs they belong to, and on and on. In case one does not recognize this, it is called racial discrimination. What would be illegal if done in an official public capacity, is done constantly in people's own lives. It is obvious, therefore, that when left to their own devices — without the long intrusive arm of government dictating what they do — people will make their decisions based on racial preference. Not even the most devout white liberals, who claim to love multiculturalism and extol integration as vitally important, would buy a home and live with their children in a black neighborhood. When it hits close to home, these white liberals demonstrate a grasp of reality in complete contradiction to what they profess to believe.

Most people in public life regard race as a subject so disagreeable and sordid that it should be ignored. But as the most pressing problem in American society, solutions will never be reached without genuine honest discussion.

Are All Cultures Equal?

The multicultural madness that has infested American education and society at large has given rise to phenomena called cultural and moral relativism. These peculiar notions maintain that *all* cultures should not only be equally celebrated in the United States (at the expense of our Western European culture), but that all cultures are equally deserving of respect and appreciation. These phenomena include the belief that all cultures are equally moral and valid. By definition, cultural and moral relativism require a deliberate refusal to make moral distinctions between Western culture, of which American culture is a part, and customs, practices and "accomplishments" that normal Americans historically have considered immoral and repellent.

Immigrants to the United States now come overwhelmingly from non-Western third world countries, and an examination of the cultures of their homelands reveals many of the bizarre cultural practices these groups have brought with them. Cultures, whether historic or current, certainly tell a story about a people. In this case, they also tell us a great deal about those Americans who demand that we accept and appreciate such cultures.

This strange desire to show "sensitivity" to other cultures has manifested itself in some shocking ways. When a Chinese immigrant beat his wife to death with a hammer for being unfaithful, New York Judge Edward Pincus sentenced him to probation only, citing "cultural differences" as an excuse for the man's atrocity. In San cisco last summer, statutory rape charges were dropped against an Iraqi native who had sex with an 11 year old (an accepted practice in Iraq) because the District Attorney "did not want to put the man's culture on trial."

Since 1965, Africa has become a measurable source of immigrants, and we are brow-beaten into "respecting" African culture. So what are Africa's current norms and historic culture? Female genital mutilation remains a custom in much of the Dark Continent. Gross national product per person is less than $200 a year. Africans have never built a modern economy. While the total number of children, grandchildren and great-grand children that the average American woman will have is 14, the equivalent figure for the average African woman is 258!

Before European colonization, no African society had devised a written language or discovered the wheel. None had a calendar or built multi-story buildings. They could not domesticate animals and had never produced a mechanical device. Africans had no concept of the biological origins of disease and attributed personal misfortunes to the work of evil spirits. Similarly, before the European conquest of the New World, many Indians practiced infant sacrifice and had not discovered the wheel.

Today, the Laotian custom of kidnapping child-brides is practiced in the United States. Voodoo and witchcraft are now practiced to such a large degree in American cities with populations from Mexico, Central America and the Caribbean, that numerous stores have emerged that carry everything needed to cast a spell, remove a hex or heal a mental disorder.

The courthouse in Dade County, Florida is constantly littered with dead animals, offered as ritual sacrifice by the city's Caribbean population as part of the practice called Santeria. Dead chickens, goat heads and lizards with their mouths tied shut are swept up daily by maintenance workers dubbed the "Voodoo Squad." Local Americans tried to charge the practitioners of these barbaric acts with animal cruelty, but the courts, citing "cultural respect," ruled them protected forms of religion.

Practitioners of something called "Palo Mayombe" rob graves and medical warehouses for human organs, mutilate and drink the blood of tortured animals and especially prize human sex organs, which they believe give them special powers. There have even been reported cases of human sacrifice.

Author Wayne Lutton writes, "That pre-modern people engage in practices Westerners find odd, repellent, or illegal is nothing new. What is remarkable is that we allow people who indulge in such practices to be imported by the millions into our country. What we are witnessing is the creation of a new doctrine: that the alleged needs of people bred to other norms give them the right to violate ours."

Perhaps even more remarkable is the obscene pursuit on the part of multiculturalist fanatics to instruct our students and citizens of their obligation to respect and appreciate all cultures as equally valid with our own. Their refusal to acknowledge, in the face of common sense and decency, the overwhelming evidence of the superiority of Western culture is yet another example of the moral decay brought about by politically correct degenerates.

Diversity is Our Weakness

The expression "Diversity is our strength" has become so ingrained in the national language that it could be mistaken for an amendment to the Constitution. Ruth Messinger was only the latest politician to say it. But they all say it. President Clinton has said "cultural diversity helps to make our nation great... America is stronger because of this diversity." Sadly, this silly mantra is not solely the province of droopy liberals. Colin Powell said it during his speech at the Republican National Convention. Dan Quayle has also said it. Never have so many people espoused something that is so obviously false.

The problem with the idea that diversity is a strength is not only that there is absolutely no evidence to substantiate it, but that *all the evidence supports the exact opposite conclusion.* Even the most cursory glance at life in America reveals that diversity is a weakness, a hindrance and a terrible burden.

A report written by the New York State Education Department refers to the ever-growing ethnic and racial diversity of the student body as "a great potential strength." In the very same report, the authors complain that schools with high percentages of minorities experience higher rates of teacher turnover, lower student scores on State tests, fewer students taking Regents courses, and a higher annual dropout rate. Clearly, once the obligatory blather about diversity being a "strength" is out of the way, the report articulates the obvious: diversity lowers standards, is very costly and is an educational burden. Because of diversity, educators are forced to develop different instructional methods, tens of millions of dollars are spent on worthless bilingual education programs, and violence and friction among ethnic groups becomes widespread. Some strength.

Diversity is said to be an important strength for America as technology brings us to a "global society" and as the world becomes more "international." People from around the world will have more contact with each other and the advantages of diversity will become obvious. But this is actually an argument *against* national diversity because it is an admission that it is difficult for different peoples — of different languages and different cultures — to communicate with each other. It is an admission, for example, that a Japanese immigrant can more easily communicate with Japan. It is an admission that people are more comfortable with and can relate more easily to people like themselves. It is an admission that diversity presents problems which can only be cured by non-diversity.

Much is frequently said about the advantages of a "diverse workforce." Blacks demand more black police officers to patrol their neighborhoods; other minorities fight for more teachers of their own race and ethnicity as role models. Both demands are premised on the grounds that these officers and teachers can better relate to their own people. Again, this is an acknowledgment that diversity does not work and that people are more trusting of members of their own race.

Because of diversity, the United States government has created the Civil Rights Commission, the Equal Employment Opportunity Commission, the Office of Federal Contract Compliance, the Justice Department's Civil Rights Division and others. Private companies have diversity managers, "sensitivity training," and affirmative action officers. All of these costly and ridiculous entities exist as an acknowledgment that a diverse work force is a constant source of friction. None would be said to be necessary in a homogeneous society. It is a very odd "strength" that needs the creation of huge bureaucratic apparatuses to keep it in line.

Ethnic tensions, be it between blacks and Korean shop owners or the Hispanic students who protested because of resentment over Black History Month, are among the many wonders of the diversity that is supposed to be a strength. Discrimination lawsuits, similarly, become a part of the day-to-day existence of corporate America only because of the existence of diversity.

Diversity is also said to bring "cultural enrichment" to America. If that is really the case, then why do people have to be forced to "enrich" themselves? Why do white Americans move in record numbers away from the very locales where immigrants and other minorities habitat?

In his landmark essay, "The Myth of Diversity", the incomparable best-selling author Jared Taylor writes, "The idea that diversity is a strength is not merely a myth, but a particularly transparent one... a perfect example of an assertion, for purely ideological reasons, of something obviously untrue."

In order to deal effectively with a problem, the first step is to acknowledge reality. By pretending diversity is a strength when it is obviously a weakness assures that misguided policies will continue.

Wither Washington?

The headline jumped off the front page of the *New York Times* last week, which automatically made it international news. "Blacks Strip Slaveholders' Names Off Schools" was the banner which confirmed, yet again, that anti-Americans exhibit no compunction and no shame when it comes to tearing down America's heroes. For it was the desecration of George Washington, the most important person in our history, that made this such a landmark story. That an *American* school in a major *American* city could remove the Father of Country's name from a place of stature — with virtually no opposition — should send shivers down the spines of patriotic Americans.

That a figure so central to the United States could be mistreated in such an official and public manner will not only disturb Eurocentrists, but may even jar some sense into naive multiculturalists as to the real agenda behind the new revisionist history. The New Orleans school, which is 98 percent black, was merely following a policy which has been in place for five years throughout the entire 91 percent black district. The school has been renamed after Charles Richard Drew, a black surgeon. The district previously removed the name of Robert E. Lee in favor of black astronaut Ronald McNair. Once again, where blacks have controlling power, it becomes obvious that race is paramount and informs every important and symbolic decision. American icons are shown utter contempt and disdain, without a peep of protest. Visualize the national din if an all-white district removed the name of Martin Luther King from a school because of a policy stating no one should be honored who cavorted with communists.

It is often considered bad manners to suggest that some blacks are somehow "less American" or unpatriotic. But it becomes infinitely more difficult to criticize such suggestions when it is *blacks themselves*, through their own words and actions, who confirm this. Carl Galmon, whom the *Times* identified as "a longtime civil rights leader" in New Orleans said, "To African-Americans, George

Washington has about as much meaning as David Duke."

Sickening words, yet very revealing. In actuality, it comes as no surprise that the black point of view is monolithic in the New Orleans school district. One would be hard-pressed to find an all-black district anywhere in the United States which did not support the dismantling of George Washington with unanimity. Several years ago, in the well-publicized National Survey of Black Americans, blacks were asked whether they felt closer to black people in Africa or their fellow white Americans. 56 percent said they felt closer to black Africans, 20 percent said neither or both and 24 percent said whites. So more than twice as many blacks responded that they felt closer to people they had never met, who speak a different language, and with whom they have nothing in common except for race.

There are countless other examples of the seemingly unbridgeable chasm between the black and white races, who so obviously live in different worlds despite the fact that they share the same citizenship. Blacks feel so alienated from the dominant culture that they constantly stake out racially exclusive organizations and subgroups such as black-only fraternities, police associations, beauty pageants and many others. There are also black-only private schools which do not recite the Pledge of Allegiance, but instead the "Pledge to African People." There is an unofficial black flag and black national anthem, "Lift Every Voice and Sing."

There are many blacks, of course, who love and embrace Western culture and have deep loyalty to the United States. Many identify more as Americans than as blacks. But most, by their own admission, do not. Even liberal writer Richard Cohen lamented the undeniable evidence, stating, "We are two nations — one black, one white."

If a nation divided against itself cannot stand, then the United States will not survive. It is certain death to tolerate the casual tearing down of George Washington. If this is permitted, if this can actually happen, why bother having a nation at all? A country that does not value its heroes and history and allows such heresy is committing national suicide. What other nation would tolerate it?

Immigration policies have added other groups to the historical black-white mix in America. All are following the lead of blacks and are behaving in the same anti-American manner — demanding special curriculum, besmirching American legends, renaming schools, and refusing to learn English. That we are losing our spine — and our nation — was articulated recently by New Yorker Sol Stern of the *City Journal*, who wrote, "My third-grader knew all about Martin Luther King but, when I asked him whether he had ever been taught about George Washington, he looked at me in all innocence and asked: 'George Washington Carver?'"

They are laughing in New Orleans.

Are All Men Created Equal?

"We hold these truths to be self-evident, that all men are created equal..."

The bastardization of Thomas Jefferson's words in the most cogently penned libertarian Declaration ever, ranks as one of the most offensive intellectual heists in American history. For it has been Marxists and other radical egalitarians who professed to be following the ideals of Jefferson when they embarked upon, and continue to saddle America, with the "civil rights" movement and its horrible offspring.

The very notion of "equality" and the context in which it is spoken can be very slippery. The historical record shows clearly that Jefferson did not believe these words literally. This was well understood in his time. When the Founding Fathers were painstakingly creating the American nation, they were guided by John Locke's ideas of liberty. As devout believers, they were also guided by traditional Christian thought.

Therefore, they believed that all men were equal in only two ways. First, they maintained that all men were equal when standing before the throne of God at the Last Judgement. Second, they held that all men were equal in the eyes of the law. Never was Jefferson's statement intended to be interpreted to mean equality in a worldly sense. It would have been a nonsensical idea to Jefferson that all men were of equal intelligence or equal ability. In fact, the Declaration of Independence was actually derived from Jefferson's fellow Virginian, George Mason, who authored the Virginia Declaration of Rights, ratified May 6, 1776.

Mason wrote, "All men are by nature equally free and independent, and have certain inherent rights, of which, when they enter into a state of society, they cannot, by any compact, derive or divest their posterity..." The distinction "equally free" (which Jefferson meant) from "created equal" has profound implications. The belief was that this condition of freedom (equal *opportunity*) would necessarily produce inequality, since men differed in inherent intelligence and ability. This inequality of results, which will invariably occur when there is equality of opportunity, is the antithesis of the guiding principle of today's liberal philosophy. Egalitarians view inequality of results as poison.

All of this would be nothing more than a historical and intellectual exercise if not for the serious policy implications of today. If policymakers' basic premise is wrong, all that follows will be devastatingly flawed. Social policies like affirmative action are based on the premise that all people are equal in ability but because of "racism," minorities are deprived of positions which they would otherwise attain. In education, an idiotic concept called "outcome-based education", which has taken root all over the country, is based on the idea that no one child is smarter than any other child. The curriculum is dumbed down to such an extent that the same "outcomes" result from all children.

If this sounds like Animal Farm, it is. Marxism, socialism and the American brand of liberalism all share the same ancestors. While these philosophies have been rejected in Eastern Europe after decades of oppression, they are alive and well in the hollow minds of American liberals who still control social, economic and educational policy. That is why the "civil rights" movement uses expressions like "economic justice." What they are after is not equal opportunity, but special privilege; not equal treatment, but a transfer of wealth from the productive to the leaches; not a strong workforce, but a racially diverse, yet weaker one.

The idea that all men are created equal is not only contradicted by science and history, but by one's own senses. Discussions of racial or ethnic inequality are so charged that they often lead to suggestions of racial superiority. But the acknowledgment of racial *differences* does not necessarily translate into "superiority." Even the Bible makes no statement on the equality of people. It is quite true that the fraudulent "Christianity" of Marxist outfits like the World Council of Churches spout the politically correct line about "equality," and are often taken by the media to be speaking for Christianity. This has given many Americans the misguided idea that Christianity suffers from the disease of modern liberalism.

This dishonest treatment of Christianity is no different than the deliberate misinterpretation of Jefferson. Father James Thornton of the True Orthodox Church writes, "That human beings are intellectually equal, or that such differences that do exist in individuals or groups are rooted, for example, in economic deprivation, would have been preposterous notions to most traditional Christian thinkers of past ages. Christianity is clearly not a religion of earthly egalitarianism."

The traditional American view is that all men possess a divine spark, the *Imago Dei*, the special dignity reserved for all children of God, each unique in his abilities, but certainly not created equal. Liberalism rejects this view. And America suffers from the disastrous policies resulting from liberalism's warped ideology.

Animal Rights Terrorists

Now that deer hunting season has arrived in New York State and Thanksgiving turkeys await millions of American holiday celebrants, the onslaught of terror from the "Bambi brigade," otherwise known as animal rights activists, has begun full throttle. It is no overstatement to label these fanatics as terrorists, since criminal activity certainly underscores one of the most bizarre ideologies and movements in the United States.

The actions and beliefs of animal rights terrorists and their propaganda organs such as People for the Ethical Treatment of Animals (PETA) are so far removed from the mainstream, that their only defense in a court of law would be criminal insanity. Under the guise of protecting defenseless species from inhumane treatment at the hands of sinister humans, groups such as the Animal Liberation Front (ALF) have vandalized laboratories which conduct animal research for the development of cures for Infant Death Syndrome, heart disease, cancer and AIDS.

Medical research using live animals has been profoundly crucial to developing vaccines for diptheria, polio, measles, mumps, whooping cough and rubella. It has also helped eradicate smallpox and control diabetes. The development of powerful antibiotics, cardiac pacemakers, microsurgery to attach severed limbs and organ transplants are all the result of animal research. Thanks to this work, the cure rate among children with leukemia has risen to greater than 70 percent.

But the animal rights terrorists do not care. Ingrid Newkirk of PETA says, "Arson, property destruction, burglary and theft are acceptable crimes when used for the animal's cause." Indeed, if one doubts her sincerity, consider that these radical groups also vandalize restaurants that sell meat products, threaten hunters in the field, steal incubators and x-ray machines from labs, drive spikes into roadways to halt hunting vehicles and attack fishermen and furriers.

They have engaged in the firebombing of supermarkets and retail stores which sell furs. According to Newkirk, "Even if the use of animals in biomedical research were to produce a cure for AIDS, we'd be against it." She even compares the preparation for Thanksgiving to the Nazi Holocaust. "Six million people died in concentration camps," she says. "But six billion broiler chickens will die this year in slaughterhouses." Eating meat, of course, is an unconscionable taboo — "primitive, barbaric, arrogant" — according to Newkirk.

PETA actually put out some ridiculous propaganda regarding turkeys, claiming their "throats are slit only partially during the slaughter process, leaving many fully conscious as they bleed to death even as they are submerged into scalding water." Ouch!

Nonsense, says the National Turkey Federation, stating "Most turkeys are raised in climate-controlled sheds, where they roam freely." The PETA claim "makes poor business sense," according to NTF. "As each turkey moves into the processing plant, an electric plate above its head shocks it, rendering the foul unconscious, hence pain-free."

Outdoors columnist Ken Moran of the *New York Post* reports that PETA's lies now include a "fact sheet" which intends to push the outlawing of fishing. Claiming that fish "feel pain," the report states that fish "often risk their own lives to aid others in trouble." According to Moran, "This is the bull you have to put up with, and the sad part, some of the public buys into this bull."

The ideology of animal rights activists is so extreme that the one constant in their philosophy is that animals are the moral equivalent of human beings. "A rat is a pig is a dog is a boy," they say.

Not only is hunting part of man's natural and historic role, it is also Biblical and an important aspect of American culture. All self-respecting and law-abiding hunters reject unnecessary cruelty to animals and do not condone unethical hunting practices. Moreover, the best way to preserve wildlife populations and endangered species is through sound restoration efforts, which are underwritten by hunting license fee revenues. Hunting, therefore, is the most humane way to control wildlife populations, which would otherwise starve painfully to death.

The benefits of medical animal research speak for themselves. While radical animal rights extremists want equal rights for cockroaches, their ideology should be dismissed as pure insanity. Their actions and behavior, however, should be taken seriously by simple dint of the damage they inflict and the terror they betray. As law-breakers, their nonsense should not be tolerated. Through their terrorism and outlaw tactics, they make the anti-gun crowd seem tame and reasonable by comparison. And that is almost an impossible accomplishment.

The Myth of Integration

There are few ideas in American history more preposterous than the 40-year struggle for racial integration. The integrationist experiment is certainly the most peculiar of movements, since it has almost always been a movement *without followers.* The idea of integration is a farce, both in principle and in practice. That axiom is quite simple — no one really believes in integration and virtually no one practices it.

Of course, there are many people who *pretend* to believe in integration, most notably white liberals. The transparency of this belief, however, is embarrassingly evident by the fact that while white liberals have always pushed integration on the rest of society, they maintain their homes and children in safe, lily-white neighborhoods. And therein lies the sin. It is not the self-segregation of white liberals that is wrong, but the hypocrisy.

On a purely moral level, integration is neutral. Moralizing whites insist that it is a moral imperative. But integration does not work because no one really wants it; and, when it is tried, it always fails. Blacks, to their credit, are now unfettered by integrationist nonsense. Even the NAACP recently acknowledged that integration — as an end in itself — is not necessarily a good thing.

The persistence with which fanatics hold to certain creeds, in the face of mountains of evidence of failure, is beyond belief. President Clinton's Initiative on Race, which purported to be an open, honest dialogue, has shown itself to be nothing more than a group of trained seals spouting the tired dogma and bromides about the vital importance of integration. In 1954, when arguing for school desegregation, Thurgood Marshall opined that all American schools would be integrated within five years and the nation as a whole within ten. Forty-five years later, the country is more segregated than ever. The reason integration has failed is because the very concept is based on one fatally flawed assumption: race doesn't matter and the races are interchangeable. Of course, on an individual level and when functioning in the real world, all Americans understand that this is nonsense. When leading their own lives, whites react in a perfectly natural and normal way to racial change and racial realities. Everyone knows this. Even Andrew Hacker, the white liberal author who blames whites for black peoples' problems, acknowledges this. He points out that when a neighborhood becomes more than ten percent black, *all* whites pick up and move. "When it comes down to it," he says, "we all behave as whites."

Left to their own devices, people will always choose to associate with their own race. That's why, in fits of tyranny, government does not leave people to their own devices. It invents forced busing and court-ordered integration. A visit to any high school or college cafeteria will show the self-segregation of the races, the obvious result of leaving people to their private choices. Ask a real estate agent if any whites are looking to move into a black neighborhood, then wait five minutes for him to stop laughing.

When it does occur, integration is always a one-way street. It is always non-whites moving into the territories of whites, not out of a principled desire to promote racial harmony, but for purely pragmatic reasons. Whites have always created the most desirable societies, neighborhoods and institutions. Naturally, non-whites want to partake of that which they could not create themselves. But as they succeed and infiltrate white institutions, whites eventually flee. Non-whites then go about re-creating in their new locations the very same disagreeable circumstances they created and left in the first place.

Residential segregation is probably the most obvious proof that people are always conscious of race. At campuses across the country, students tend to apply to separate dormitories along racial lines. At Cornell, a referendum was put to students to end this practice, abolish self-segregation and allow for random housing. It was overwhelmingly defeated.

The New York City Board of Education continues to outdo itself in racial madness. Integration, apparently, is something so desirable and noble, that white parents will do anything to escape the tragic circumstances of white homogeneity and remove their children from white schools so that the kids can enjoy the glories of being surrounded by minority students. "The *Reverse* Open Enrollment Program" requires the principals of schools that are classified as "75% or more WHITE" to inform parents of this great opportunity. Schools officials maintain that *not once* in the ten years this program has been in place, have white parents opted for the glories of sending their children to non-white schools.

The strife, riots and resentments which occur wherever integration is tried or forced upon people are more than enough proof that the promise of harmonic multi-racialism can never come true. Like the promise of communism, it will wind up on the ash heap of history.

From Charity to Welfare

Americans have a history of generosity and compassion towards the truly needy that has always been balanced by a healthy skepticism of free handouts to the indigent. This proper mentality about charity served the nation well for more than a century. Until government reared its ugly head and began coercing citizens into compulsory transfer payments from the productive to the leaches, the basic view of Americans was that many of the poor were responsible for their own plights.

This assumption — that a certain segment of society would simply rather live on the dole than work — was the intellectual fulcrum on which all forms of alms were based. Effective charity, therefore, was as much the art of *withholding* as it was the art of giving. To a very large degree, the idea of charity was driven by the conviction that peoples' own vices caused poverty, so pauperism could only be cured by moral regeneration, not handouts.

In colonial times, charity was essentially private and voluntary —limited to victims of catastrophes like fires and earthquakes, when neighbors would share their homes. Private charities carefully screened out loafers and tried to find people work rather than give money. For the incurably unregenerate, there was the workhouse, the only public charity to which citizens were entitled. The workhouses were hardly the dole. A meager existence was guaranteed in exchange for work. The colonists truly believed in Second Thessalonians: "If any would not work, neither should he eat." All alms outside the workhouse were believed to be a temptation to indolence.

The American system worked so well in comparison to government-funded relief in England, that an astonished English statesman who spent two years in the United States commented that he "saw but one beggar." One 19th century charity official (who would undoubtedly be fired today amidst protests from the "civil rights" establishment) explained that the able-bodied poor "should be compelled to work or left to suffer the consequences of their misconduct." Indeed, when one Boston charity established a "work test," whereby if a man were willing to chop wood for a few hours, only then would he would be entitled to help, the "needy" fell from 160 a day to fewer than 50.

What has gone wrong? Despite the reduction in the welfare rolls and politicians making hay out of the need for "workfare," the tragedy of American compassion is distinguished by a complete reversal of the charity mentality, at least by government. The liberal definition of "compassion" is now extorting from the productive and giving to the irresponsible and the lazy. Any challenge to this state of affairs has been met with accusations of "mean-spiritedness."

So what is welfare and who is on it? The technical name of what is generally thought of as "welfare" is Aid to Families With Dependent Children (AFDC), although there are other programs that steal even more of taxpayers' dollars to give to those that did not earn it. The name is deliberately deceiving in order to give the impression that the handout is going to the children of loafers ("families") rather than the loafers themselves. Of course, the definition of "family" has lost all meaning, since more than half of the "families" receiving welfare are single women — never married — who have illegitimate children.

The average monthly AFDC case load for the country is roughly 4.8 million "families," or 15 million individuals. Payment levels and criteria differ from state to state, with the amount paid by the federal government also varying depending on how poor the state is. Nevertheless, since 90 million Americans pay federal income taxes, every six or seven taxpayers are forced to support a welfare recipient as well as themselves and their families. At any given time, an astounding 65 percent of those on the dole have been getting welfare for *more than eight years.*

Blacks are by far the most prolific abusers of the system, with 18 percent of all blacks on welfare. Ten percent of Hispanics are on the dole, while 2.9 percent of whites are. So any given black is six times as likely as a given white to be on welfare. Blacks also stay on the rolls the longest, averaging 8.14 years. This should come as no surprise since illegitimacy is the single best predictor of whether or not welfare is in a child's future. And the black illegitimacy rate is shameful, with 68 percent of black babies born out of wedlock. So not only is welfare a massive transfer of wealth, it is overwhelmingly a transfer from whites to non-whites.

Before the current government mentality regarding handouts became fashionable and there was still a stigma attached to indolence, the black family was essentially intact and illegitimacy a mere fraction of what it is today. But the incentives are now perverse. Tax laws combined with marriage make living on the dole a more prosperous situation for layabouts, leaving little incentive to get off welfare. Since all penalties — both financial and social — have been removed for reckless procreation, the productive will continue to support the dregs of society.

Beware Of Earth Day

Next month, tree huggers and other assorted environmental

wackos will once again be pouring mounds of incense on the altar of the one pagan holiday celebrated in the United States. Although organizers of Earth Day cleverly try to portray this farce as merely a celebration of green grass, clean water and legitimate pollution concerns, the actual agenda is—and always has been—nothing less than radical environmental extremism.

The original Earth Day (1970) was clearly a creation of the hard left, mobilized by anti-Vietnam War fervor. Anti-American radicals organized the Environmental Teach-In, the major Washington-based group designed to coordinate Earth Day activities nationwide. The Teach-In tactics were modeled on those of anti-war protesters. Speakers routinely used the environment as an excuse to rally activists by declaring that "racism, poverty and the Vietnam War" fell into their definition of "pollution."

Co-Chairman of the Teach-In, radical leftist Congressman Gaylord Nelson, told a group of Denver college students that the American environment is "the rats in the ghetto. It is a hungry child in a land of affluence," and that environmental problems were exacerbated "by the expenditures of $25 billion a year on the war in Vietnam, instead of our decaying, crowded, congested, polluted urban areas that are inhuman traps for millions of people."

Today, the organizers of Earth Day are many of the same people from 1970, including Nelson and the other co-chairman, former Congressman Pete McCloskey, as well as a virtual roster of '60's radicals. Lynn White, Jr. a history professor at the University of California and major Earth Day organizer believes Judaism and Christianity are responsible for the destruction of the environment because of God's commandment to man to subdue the earth. The belief that God made man in his own image makes Christianity the most "anthropocentric religion the world has ever seen." White also believes in "pagan animism," the doctrine that stones and plants have conscious life. "Christianity made it possible to exploit nature in a mood of indifference to the feelings of natural objects," he says.

Radical Bill McKibben writes in his book, *The End of Nature*, "Human happiness, and certainly human fecundity, are not as important as a wild and healthy planet. I know social scientists who remind me that people are part of nature, but it isn't true... We have become a plague upon ourselves and upon the earth. Until such time as Homo sapiens should decide to rejoin nature, some of us can only hope for the right virus to come along."

We're not just recycling! Sponsoring organizations of Earth Day like the Sierra Club and Friends of the Earth are no less extreme. David Brower, who founded Friends of the Earth and is former executive director of the Sierra Club wrote in his recent book, *For Earth's Sake*, that the deaths of young men in war are no more serious than mountains and wilderness touched by humans.

Earth First!, another Earth Day sponsor, has gone beyond extremism and into the realm of "ecoterrorism," criminal activity. Earth First!'s founder, Dave Foreman, was arrested for conspiring to sabotage an electrical power tower in Arizona. Foreman is the author of *Ecodefense: A Field Guide to Monkeywrenching*, which offers detailed advice on how to sabotage development, including power lines. Ecoterrorism also involves the spiking of trees with metal spikes, puncturing the tires of off-road vehicles and the destruction of bridges. John Davis, the editor of Earth First!'s newsletter, asserts, "Human beings, as a species, have no more value than slugs."

Earth Day supporter Michael Lerner has written that Earth First! "has had a positive impact. That sentiment seems to be shared by many in the Sierra Club, the National Audubon Society and other mainstream environmental groups." Mainstream? All, like Earth First!, are Earth Day sponsors. Co-Chairman Gaylord Nelson says, "I think groups like Greenpeace and Earth First! make a significant contribution to the educational process."

Incredibly, many of these groups have been kept alive with taxpayer funds through federal grants.

Despite this madness, even legitimate concerns over the preservation of America's parks, lakes and wilderness are nothing more than sky-is-falling claptrap from Al Gore and tree-worshipping zealots. The global warming "menace" has been proven a fraud. Federal parklands in the United States have jumped some 30 million acres since 1970, according to *U.S. News & World Report.* Levels of pollutant gases in the air have decreased dramatically. Forest land has increased some 25 percent since 1952. Rivers, streams and lakes are also cleaner.

Nevertheless, here comes Earth Day, another excuse for the radical left to worship (and smoke) grass.

Multicultural Madness

The specter of multiculturalism in American society can only be categorized as an assault on Western civilization. With its inherent anti-Americanism, it manifests itself in ways that are not in the least bit subtle. The gradual tearing down of all that America has ever stood for and accomplished, and the vilification of persons and institutions America has always revered are the ultimate goals of multiculturalism. Conquest not by military triumph, but by cultural assassination.

At the Smithsonian Institution, demands are made that cowboys be presented as merciless killers; at universities, the strange concept of Afro-centrism imparts that Moses and Cleopatra were black; also, the display of the American flag during the Gulf War is considered "offensive" speech; in sports, fans of the Atlanta Braves are chastised for cheering on their team with the "tomahawk chop" and the famed St. John's University basketball team is forced to change its name from the Redmen to the Red Storm. All politically correct sacrifices at the altar of multiculturalism.

Some of these assaults are symbolic and are directed at the American soul, which has always had a Eurocentric core. Others are more tangible, such as the demand for bilingual education and the rewriting of school textbooks. But in whatever guise it appears, multiculturalism in its essence refers to a radical revision of history.

Nowhere does multiculturalism present a greater danger than in American public schools, where even the youngest of students are indoctrinated in anti-Americanism. The underlying philosophy of multiculturalism is: Western culture and civilization are evil and historically exploitative. This ideology, taken to its logical conclusion, reveals itself in a hysterical collection of grievances from so-called oppressed minorities against the white race and the societies they have created.

The New York State Department of Education, in its official statement endorsing multicultural education, states that non-whites "have all been the victims of an intellectual and educational oppression that has characterized the culture and institutions of the United States and the European American world for centuries." The appointed panel overseeing and approving New York's multicultural curriculum program included Leonard Jeffries, the black supremacist State University professor who states that blacks are the superior "sun people" because of the melanin in their skin, and whites are the inferior "ice people."

In San Francisco, the school board voted to require the reading of non-white authors, as well as writers who are "lesbian, gay, bisexual and transgender." The new requirement rebukes Mark Twain for his alleged disrespect of blacks. No more Huck Finn.

White educators who support multiculturalism in the schools — either by their silence or by overt advocacy — are a combination of the ignorant and the cowardly. In either case, they are complicit in the spread of this grotesque malignancy.

So the expression "celebrating diversity" really means rejoicing in the dispossession and declining influence of white Americans and the historical culture they have built. For expedient political purposes, multiculturalists (and some naive fools who Lenin referred to as "useful idiots") sometimes pretend that multiculturalism is merely a benign "respect" for different cultures (as if all cultures are deserving of respect). But the obvious aim is the total destruction of Western culture by replacing it with a venomous anti-Western philosophy.

It is now a commonplace that the greatness of the Founding Fathers is called into question. George Washington is more often portrayed as an evil slaveholder in the public schools. Even the most trivial accomplishments of non-whites are given primary stature. Less than one-third of American 17 year olds know in what historical time frame the American Revolution took place. But they are inundated with knowledge of the Ku Klux Klan.

The United States is the only nation foolish enough to tolerate such a cultural emasculation. Non-whites clamor for multiculturalism only when they are in the minority numerically. When they are in the majority, their institutions fervently protect their racial and cultural exclusivity. No one could trick historically black colleges in the United States or nations like Mexico or Guatemala into "celebrating diversity."

No self-respecting nation would tolerate a cultural takeover, let alone the type that blames its own people for all the ills that have beset mankind. Yet that is exactly what is happening. By definition, different historical points of view translate into multiple national identities. Washington cannot be a hero and a terrorist at the same time. Non-white alien radicals and their multiculturalist partisans in the schools understand this completely — and are exploiting white liberal guilt to the hilt. A nation that tries to stand for everything, stands for nothing — and will dissolve due to its own suicidal cowardice.

What is Racism?

Although "racism" is by far the greatest sin a white person can commit, according to the liberal intelligentsia, and the perpetrator of an alleged racist act faces the most brutal response imaginable, the term "racism" is no longer overtly defined.

The probable reason for this is that the definition itself has evolved to fit left-wing cultural guidelines. The more outrageous the actions and demands of non-whites and their partisans, the broader the definition necessarily had to become.

There are several definitions of racism. As the term has

traditionally been understood, it meant actions, statements, beliefs or policies which were untrue or motivated by falsehoods, and which unjustly discriminated against persons on account of race. (This actually defines affirmative action, preferences, set-asides and quotas, but don't tell anyone.)

Forbes magazine senior editor Peter Brimelow says the new definition of a racist is anyone winning an argument with a liberal. It is difficult to argue with that conclusion, given the reckless manner in which the word is thrown around. Certainly, Brimelow is correct in that the traditional definition no longer applies.

The columnist Joseph Sobran pointed out several years ago how the term "McCarthyism" evolved from its original meaning. After the spectacular hearings of Senator Joseph McCarthy and the blacklists, the expression "McCarthyism" came into wide use in America. It meant, quite simply, falsely accusing someone of being a communist. When the New Left took over American culture, the term came to mean *any* accusation of communist ties, *even if it was true*. In fact, the definition went even further to describe as "McCarthyism" any true assertion of a person being a communist, *even if the person accused admitted it*. In other words, it was simply bad manners to call someone a communist and anyone who did it was a "McCarthyite."

Such is the case with "racism." For practical purposes, the only definition that really matters is as the term is used in contemporary cultural and political jargon. Since the traditional understanding of the concept no longer exists, it has become necessary for the Thought Police who work overtime catching those rascally racists to expand the definition of the term. Therefore, it is now "racist" to point out inconvenient and uncomfortable facts about non-whites, even if no one disputes their veracity.

For example, to cite police and government statistics which make crystal clear the fact that violent street crime in American cities is overwhelmingly a black phenomenon is to commit a "racist" act. To point out—without a trace of malice—that non-white test scores and scholastic achievements do not measure up to those of whites is also racist.

So in order to not be a racist, one is *required* to ignore the evidence, not to mention one's own senses. To avoid charges of racism, one must cease to educate and inform oneself of the pertinent facts needed to arrive at an intelligent conclusion. This is what Aldous Huxley called "vincible" ignorance, which is when the facts are so unpleasant that "we don't know because we don't want to know."

The definition of "racism" has also been expanded to mean opposition — no matter how well thought out and factually documented — to the ever-increasing and radical demands of minority fanatics. A principled opposition to affirmative action is, therefore, an act of racism.

The accusation is used so irresponsibly that even George Bush, one of the most racially nervous and moderate Republicans around, felt its wrath. Here was a man who infuriated conservatives by signing the 1991 Civil Rights Act into law (which even Ed Koch acknowledged was a quota bill.) When his black Assistant Secretary of Education, Michael Williams, bravely announced that scholarship money set aside for minorities was illegal, Bush forced Williams to withdraw his ruling. Yet when Bush was less than forthcoming with federal aid for the district which non-whites destroyed during the Rodney King riots, radical black Congresswoman Maxine Waters accused him of guess what. More recently, Calvin Butts, a Harlem clergyman, accused Rudy Giuliani of racism for similarly absurd reasons.

The term "prejudiced" was once a fashionable substitute for "racism" and literally means to pre-judge something — to reach a conclusion without examining the facts involved. But again, of course, liberals have turned this definition on its ear since, by their definition, one is prejudiced or "racist" for examining the facts *too closely.*

"Racism," therefore, is a liquid concept, subject to the changing ideological fanaticism of non-white radicals (who themselves, of course, can never be racist.) It will mean something different tomorrow than it means today, depending on the whims and desires for racial spoils always extracted at the expense of whites and resulting in the dispossession of whites — and the inevitable opposition to these demands. And, perhaps most tragically, there will always be an abundance of terrified whites who will assent and go along with this dastardly con game.

Those Pesky North Asians

Listening to the radical non-white interest groups who enjoy the benefits of citizenship in a country they are always disparaging, one would believe that American history has been one of constant racial discrimination, repression of minorities and other sordid acts and sins committed by the dominant white hegemony.

For practical purposes, it is irrelevant that most Americans do not actually believe this and that it is untrue. What matters is that the United States government believes it. Certainly, with the invention of affirmative action, anti-discrimination laws, multiculturalism, forced integration, bilingual education, ad nauseam, the elected government operates in a perpetual state of racial atonement. When black and Hispanic hustlers give orders, the American government almost always acquiesces in fear.

There is one group, however, that has consistently succeeded in America despite many historical obstacles and official acts of racial discrimination. North Asians — Chinese, Japanese and Koreans — have not only surpassed all other groups (including whites) in many areas, but have done so quietly, without complaining that past acts of discrimination entitle them to special treatment. A look at history reveals that North Asians, at the very least, could point to very specific wrongs committed against their ancestors. At worst, they could make the same types of outrageous demands other non-white groups use to shake down the American taxpayer. More often than not, they simply go about their business without allowing the past to shackle them, physically or psychologically.

While blacks were permitted to become citizens in 1870, Asians were barred from naturalization until 1943. Chinese began coming to the United States in 1850 and had, therefore, to wait almost 100 years for citizenship. California's Constitution of 1879 denied the vote to "natives of China, idiots and insane persons." (Which would also have denied citizenship to most of today's Congress.) In 1914, the U.S. Supreme Court ruled that citizenship could be denied to foreign-born Asians. In 1855, because of Chinese willingness to work for low wages, the legislature levied a $55 per person entry tax on Chinese immigrants and eventually barred all people of "Mongolian" descent from entering the state except in cases of shipwreck, after which survivors were expelled upon recovering.

California then passed a tax on foreign miners which was only enforced against Chinese. A $2.50 monthly tax was assessed on all Chinese over the age of 18 who were not producing sugar, rice, coffee or tea. Fees were levied on laundries that did not use a vehicle — a deliberate attack on Chinese laundries. Chinese who sold vegetables suddenly had to get a license when no one else had to. From 1854 to 1874, Chinese could not testify as witnesses against whites. After the Civil War, Chinese coolies were being bought and sold like animals in Caribbean "man markets."

Although Japanese arrived more recently — beginning in 1885 — they were greeted with similar laws. While the Chinese were close to being granted citizenship in 1941, Japanese-Americans were stripped of their civil rights soon after Pearl Harbor. They were rounded up and sent behind barbed wire in concentration camps. If any American group had the right to live in bitterness it would be the Japanese. But rather than be shackled by the past, within 25 years of this atrocity, Japanese had incomes 32 percent above the national average. If this internment had happened to blacks, Americans would be hearing about it daily for the next 500 years.

Today, North Asians who have arrived so recently speaking no English, usually graduate from high school a few years later at the top of their classes. Incredibly, by 1965 Chinese and Japanese had higher average incomes than native-born whites. Not a day goes by without reading about North Asians blowing out the competition in science contests. Asians from the poorest families score higher on the Standard Aptitude Test than blacks from the *highest* economic levels. North Asians are now hurt almost as much as whites by affirmative action.

Miserable black test scores on standardized tests are often attributed to "cultural bias," begging the answer to why North Asians score as high as whites. The North Asian crime rate is so low as to be almost non-existent. Although Korean grocery stores create retail trade and save desolate streets from evaporating, they are often greeted with hostility in black neighborhoods.

It is a fact that the extraordinary success of North Asians in the United States serves as one of the most powerful threats to the notion that incessant white racism holds back minorities. The presence of North Asians creates a very awkward and inconvenient obstacle to the race hustlers and shakedown artists who constantly demand redress for historical grievances rather than take responsibility for their own failures.

Why Race Hoaxes Are Common

The Tawana Brawley circus has finally concluded after more than ten years of vaudeville, and although this particular charade became the most notorious racial hoax in America, it is far from a solitary incident. So how common are racial hoaxes, who commits them and why?

Since America is obsessed with thought crimes, and "racism" surpasses all of them, physical crimes of a racial nature — "hate crimes" — most sufficiently satisfy the hunger of race hustlers and ivory tower white liberals for more "proof" of rampant bigotry. Genuine crimes that are motivated by racial animus become national news, which is why there is so much currency in perpetrating hoaxes. The windfall from a successfully orchestrated hoax can be fame, money and an inordinate amount of public sympathy. Rodney King, with his IQ of 65, criminal record and drunken driving, is now a millionaire because the media played up his story as a racial incident.

The different races derive different benefits from racial hoaxes and their motivations are also dissimilar. Blacks by far perpetrate the greatest number of hoaxes. Surprisingly, although some false claims have been made for the purpose of "verifying" white racism and as tools for black resistance, most blacks contrive stories of race bias crimes in order to simply cover up their own misdeeds. By now, it is well-known that Tawana Brawley lied not out of any implacable hatred of whites, but for fear that her step-father would beat her for not arriving home on time.

This is a very common pattern among black hoaxers. In 1990, Sabrina Collins repeatedly vandalized her own dormitory at Emory University. By claiming whites had done it, she received an outpouring of public sympathy. It was discovered she faked the incident to divert attention from the fact that she had been accused of cheating on an exam.

Other incidents reported to the police reveal that black criminals have carved "KKK" on their victims to throw investigators off the scent. The tactic is successful because the political desire to highlight white racism is so high.

According to Laird Wilcox in his book *Crying Wolf: Hate Crime Hoaxes in America*, Jewish hoaxers are the most ideological, rarely perpetrating racial scams to cover their own crimes, but usually to heighten awareness of "anti-Semitism." Jews who spray paint swastikas on synagogues are usually fanatics constantly needing to show evidence that the world hates them.

These scams pay such dividends that even non-Jews find them appealing. One man set fire to his own house and told police it was the work of anti-Semites who *thought* he was Jewish. Perhaps the most interesting story is the strange case of a true anti-Semite in Salem, Massachusetts who was caught *painting over* anti-Semitic graffiti on a synagogue for fear that Jews would use it to their advantage.

In the rare instances when whites perpetrate hoaxes by falsely accusing blacks, the motivation is never to claim being the victims of black racism or for public sympathy. Rather, it is purely utilitarian. To cover their own crimes, whites blame blacks because it is so plausible and believable. The two most well-known white hoaxers are Susan Smith of South Carolina, who murdered her two small sons by pushing her car into the river with the boys strapped inside and then blamed a black man; and Charles Stuart, who shot his pregnant wife for insurance money and then shot himself, later claiming that a black had attacked them.

There is no real benefit in claiming to be the victim of black racism since such incidents are always downplayed and an extraordinary effort is made by media and politicians to deny racial motivations in blacks, even in the face of clear evidence. White victims of black racism are not made into celebrities and are not then designated "spokesmen" for a noble cause.

Conversely, the national splash, guilt-ridden editorials and collective breast-beating that follow incidents of alleged white racism, and the desire to focus on white bias, are so extreme and hysterical that they continue full throttle *even after the hoax has been revealed and the incident proven false*. When Tawana Brawley was exposed, the leftist *Nation* magazine said that it didn't matter whether the incident actually happened or not. The hoax served a useful purpose since black women are constantly abused by white men.

Radical lawyer William Kunstler said, "It makes no difference anymore whether the attack on Tawana really happened... a lot of black women are treated the way she says she was." When Sabrina Collins' hoax was exposed, Otis Smith of the Atlanta chapter of the NAACP said, "It doesn't matter to me whether she did it or not, because of all the pressure these black students are under at these predominantly white schools. If this will highlight it, if it will bring it to the attention of the public, I have no problem with that."

The fact is that bias crimes perpetrated by whites are extremely rare. Radical groups like the NAACP need to invent them in order to justify their organization's continued contemptuous existence. They will stop at nothing, not even supporting the fabricated tales of liars. Likewise, America's cultural climate requires that these "incidents" be highlighted to conform to the racial madness that has become a national obsession.

Pledging Allegiance to Whom?

With Flag Day and Independence Day bringing out the American flags, and the intervening period between the two holidays designated as an official time of national reflection, the issue of defining patriotism has come to the fore.

Panelists on the *Jim Lehrer Newshour* struggled with the concept on the eve of the Fourth of July, with all finally agreeing that patriotism is not what it once was, that many Americans lack the feeling that captured their countrymen even as recently as a generation ago. The panel, which included former Georgia Senator Sam Nunn, stressed economic and community issues. The more involved in the community, the more patriotic people tend to be, they opined. Similarly, they concluded, economics plays a significant role in patriotism since favorable economic times make people feel good about the country, while the struggle in bad times also plays a role in people's attitudes.

Not once in the entire discussion were the roles of ethnicity, immigration and race mentioned, making the assemblage of the panel, ultimately, an effort in futility. To ignore those issues on the subject of lack of patriotism is on the order of discussing the NBA finals without once mentioning the factor of Michael Jordan.

Feelings of patriotism and nationalism, of course, transcend economics. The issue is innate loyalty which almost never changes. Certainly, many foreigners that have made a success of their lives here are loyal to the United States. But which ones? Invariably, they are of European descent.

Blacks, who have lived in North America longer than any other group and have fought bravely in all American wars, still betray, in survey after survey, an alienness toward the United States that exceeds even that of some recently arrived immigrants. The well-publicized Survey of Black Americans found that twice as many blacks said they felt closer to blacks in Africa than to their fellow white Americans.

Regarding immigrants, Teddy Roosevelt warned against dual loyalties and stated that there was "no room for hyphenated Americans." But the matter of dual loyalty is rarely a factor anymore, since those Americans lacking patriotism have only one loyalty — and it's not to the United States.

In March, Mexico changed its constitution to grant dual nationality to all Mexicans, meaning that even Mexican-Americans born in the United States can regain their Mexican nationality since the change is retroactive. Until now, any Mexican who became a naturalized citizen of a foreign country was stripped of all rights as a Mexican. While there have been economic factors which Mexicans had to consider when deciding on pursuing American citizenship, there are none now. But, most importantly, is the factor of loyalty *of the heart* of these "Americans" ("Americans" defined, of course, as merely having the proper citizenship papers.)

Leticia Quezado, a member of a Los Angeles school board, explains, "I never stopped feeling Mexican. I have become a United States citizen because this is where I live, where I have made my professional life. I have made a commitment, but it's sort of an intellectual commitment, whereas emotionally I'm Mexican. I want to be Mexican. I feel very close to the country of my birth." Now that they will not lose the benefits of nationality, the INS expects a surge in Mexican applications for United States citizenship, so as to have the best of both economic worlds.

Likewise, the Dominican Republic has made plans to let Dominican-Americans vote in its elections in 2000. Fernando Mateo, a successful Bronx businessman, has lived almost his entire life in the United States. Still, he says, "What I want to focus on is making my country [the Dominican Republic] the best country in the world." No problem of dual loyalty there.

It is a laughable notion to think these views are somehow aberrational. They are, of course, the norm. To suggest that these "Americans" trace their lineage to and consider Washington and Jefferson their patrimony is preposterous. Donna Shalala, President Clinton's Secretary for Health and Human Services, is of Lebanese descent. "I have no affinity and feel no connection to the Pilgrims," she said. And this coming from a high-ranking official in the United States government who is in the line of succession for the presidency. A true patriot's loyalty almost never strays. Even anti-government types confine their criticism of the United States to those instances when America abandons its original ideals. It is never a matter of dual or changing allegiances. But until the government wakes up to the fact that race, ethnicity and immigration are the most crucial factors in America's survival, the country will continue down the road to oblivion. If there is doubt about this, just ask the hyphenated Americans.

The Invented Indian

While blacks are generally regarded as the recognized experts in the game of racial shakedowns, extorting money and preferential treatment as compensation for so-called past oppression, it is American Indians — one-half of one percent of the United States population — who may actually be the real geniuses at obtaining racial spoils.

The Indian lobby, taking its cue from the protracted black con job, has perfected its nefarious intimidation of the guilt-ridden pale face. What is remarkable about the stellar success of the Indian extraction of benefits is that it has been accomplished by trading on a past that never was, a past that was invented, a myth. Naturally, the propagation of the invented Indian could not have occurred without the assistance of white apologists, but like all myths, this one is dying hard.

CULTURE

The fabricated saga of the Indians, now official doctrine, offers that before the ruthless white man arrived on the shores of the Americas, "Native Americans" were spiritual, noble and wise, living in harmony with nature. Having shared their knowledge of the wilderness and enlightened the white man with their egalitarian social order and near-utopian society, Indians were thanked with enslavement, disease, genocide and the destruction of their culture. So resilient is the Indian that despite European atrocities, his spirit remains pure and his culture has survived. The Indian take on history is, orthodoxy maintains, the only accurate and acceptable one. In preparation for the quincentenary of Columbus' discovery, *National Geographic* comissioned Indians to write articles from "the most intimate — and perhaps truest — perspective of all."

Reality, very stubbornly, tells a far different story. Certainly, the Indians were dispossessed, but the way they usually conducted themselves could charitably be characterized as inhumane, or inhuman. Although cannibalism, infanticide, ritual torture, slavery, slaughter, scalping and the most gruesome forms of savagery are well-documented, these awful truths are seldom written about any more by historians.

In Canada, when work crews at ancient Indian camp sites find burnt human bones, the evidence is downplayed, so as to not reveal what this actually means. That Indians regularly attacked and killed peaceful settlers is beyond historical dispute. War, in fact, was the natural state for most Indians. Military historian John Keegan has written that cruelty in the war-making methods of some Indians "has no parallel elsewhere in the world."

In Thomas Goodrich's book *Scalp Dance: Indian Warfare on the High Plains*, he quotes Col. Henry Carrington, whose American troops were tortured and mutilated by a combined force of Sioux and Cheyenne in 1866. "Eyes torn out and laid on the rocks; noses cut off; ears cut off; chins hewn off; teeth chopped out; ...brains taken out and placed on rocks; ... hands cut off; feet cut off; arms taken out from sockets; private parts severed and indecently place on the person..."

In the aftermath of Little Bighorn, Goodrich quotes Private Jacob Adams who wrote, "The men...were...scalped and horribly mutilated. Some were decapitated, while many bodies were lacking feet..." Private Adams also described the dead as being propped up for target practice with bows and arrows.

Indians routinely took body parts as trophies and those enemies they could not torture because of quick death were horribly mutilated. Indians consistently did these things to women and children, with an American soldier witnessing a little girl tied by hands and feet, her body full of arrows and horribly mangled. Rape, torture and other unspeakable crimes were not inflicted solely on whites, but just as often on rival tribes.

The fading of the Indian way of life was, by any honest assessment, a boon to the New World. As Steven Schwamenfeld writes, it was "incompatible with civilization." Even the great Mark Twain wrote of the Indian, "He is ignoble — base and treacherous, and hateful in every way."

But with so many American intellectuals spouting the propaganda about a glorious Indian past, the Indian windfall has been steep. Since 1970, Indian law suits have attempted and often succeeded in stripping the ownership title from some 40 million acres of land in the Eastern United States. These bogus land claims, playing on public sympathy for the notion that whites "stole" the land, have appeared despite the fact that the land was legally purchased and vastly improved since the Indians lived on it. These claims have sometimes bankrupted honest American land owners.

On reservations, Indians enjoy exemptions from many taxes and laws, including $1.4 billion of American tax money a year on these "sovereign nations." The most lucrative form of unearned income they enjoy is gambling, where Las Vegas-type casinos operate tax-free outside of American law. Indians-only health and welfare benefits surpass all other handouts in their extravagance. Outside the reservation, Indians are entitled to the usual affirmative action and race-based preferences that other non-whites reap.

Not bad for a minority with a 45 percent poverty rate, 35 percent unemployment rate and the highest alcoholism rate in the world. For the invented Indian, a shakedown of historic proportions.

In Defense of Militias

A distrust of government is not only healthy, it is totally American. The Founding Fathers understood well that government, by its very nature, is tyrannical. They also understood that a strong centralized government and the disarming of its citizenry were the quickest roads to tyranny. For that reason, they stressed the idea of federalism, states' rights and local control, embodied most overtly in the Tenth Amendment. It was the belief that men could not be trusted with power that led to the complex system of checks and balances which formed the Constitution.

Much has been made of the fact that the early Americans left Europe to escape religious oppression. We learned as children that the First Amendment guaranteed us the right of free speech, freedom of assembly, and the right to petition the government for a redress of grievances. Far less has been made of the powerful motivation of the Founders to include the Second Amendment in the Constitution. It reads, "A well regulated Militia, being necessary to the security of a free State, the right of the people to keep and bear Arms, shall not be infringed."

The Founders understood that an unarmed citizenry was tantamount to an enslaved populace. Only when denied the freedom to possess arms can men be oppressed. In the Federalist Papers, which provided the raison d'etre (reasoning) for the Constitution, James Madison, the Father of the Constitution, wrote, "We will not become like the tyrannies of Europe, whose governments are afraid to trust the people with arms." Washington said, "No freeman shall be denied the use of arms." Patrick Henry said, "The great object is that every man be armed...Everyone who is able may have a gun."

Clearly, any objective and honest reading of history, especially as applied to the driving forces of ideas that led to America's founding, would have to include discussion of the right to bear arms. But what has this to do with the "militias" of today which have come under such fierce attack because of the ghastly bombing in Oklahoma City?

In general, the media have irresponsibly linked "right-wing" hate groups" with the legitimate militias which have been formed in as many as 26 states and include roughly 100,000 members. *Newsweek*, for example, ran a one-page layout of "the far right" which linked the Ku Klux Klan, the Aryan Nations, the Order and other like groups with the Michigan Militia, as if they all belong in the same category. From what is known, the Michigan Militia (whose founder is part Jewish) has no record of lawlessness whatsoever. Undoubtedly, its members are among the most law-abiding citizens in the state.

Liberals, reacting hysterically, have demonized by crude association what is certainly one of the most patriotic, peace-loving and constitutionally derived movements.

It is true, in a technical sense, that the objective of the militias -- in the most extreme circumstances -- is to do battle against the government. But those circumstances would certainly only arrive when the government was no longer legitimate. No objective, then, could be closer to the beliefs of the Founding Fathers. They made clear that the formation of militias was necessary to guard against the very government they were in the process of creating. Founder George Mason stated, "...the question then will be, whether a consolidated government can preserve the freedom and secure the rights of the people. I ask, who are the Militia? They consist now of the whole people."

It cannot be more evident that the "militias" envisioned by the founders were intended to be the common people at large, preserving liberty by acting as a check on the government. Founder Richard Henry Lee stated, "To preserve liberty, it is essential that the whole body of the people always possess arms and be taught alike, especially when young, how to use them."

Left-wing hatred of the United States is distinguished by its vitriolic abhorrence of that which is inherently American -- Western culture, Eurocentrism and Anglo-Saxon mores. On the contrary, "right-wing" distrust in government, as embodied in the views of many militia members, is profoundly *pro-American*, in the sense that government is detested only when it strays from the original American ideal -- liberty, individualism, local control and American sovereignty.

The fears that stir today's militias are not in any sense unreasonable. It is not only the anger regarding the government intruding ruthlessly on the right to bear arms. Far from it. Confiscatory taxation is, for example, justifiably viewed as a form of slavery. Today, Americans are forced to surrender an obscenely large portion of the fruits of their labor to government to use for the benefit of others who did not work for it. Certainly, the Founding Fathers would have considered any government which celebrates Tax Freedom Day (the day we begin working for ourselves and not government) as late as June to be oppressive.

Similarly, not only militias, but most Americans, are unnerved by the relinquishing of American sovereignty to the United Nations. The New World Order, in its most extreme form, is world government. Organizations like the World Trade Organization, where tiny two-bit dictatorships have veto power over U.S. trade policy, give credence to such fears. Recall that Vice President Gore commended American soldiers who gave their lives in Somalia for their "service to the United Nations." Hmmm.

Finally, government agencies which operated like rogue police in the Waco and Randy Weaver affairs, give rise to legitimate fears that the government is running roughshod over individual liberties. How many Americans really believe that the government, the way it currently operates, is really run "by the people" and "for the people"?

The circumstances under which the government would become tyrannical would, naturally, arrive incrementally. But human history is basically one of oppression. The Founding Fathers were correct in their fear of government. Their solution was to erect the most successful form of government ever, consisting not only of checks and balances, but of safeguards -- which included the Second Amendment's right of individuals to bear arms and the existence of an armed populace in the form of militias.

Curing What Ails Khalid Muhammad

In order to properly diagnose what is ailing the boisterous black supremacist Khalid Abdul Muhammad, it would be instructive to examine precisely what his gripes are. Among other things, he asserts the Mayor of New York City is a "cracker," Jews are "bloodsuckers" who move their businesses into black communities in order to cheat the locals and, in his most recent diatribe concluding the Harlem youth rally, he instructed blacks to take the billy clubs from police and "ram it up their behinds."

"Look at those bastards," he said, referring to the police. "Giuliani sics them on anybody to start riots — those bastards... If you look around you see them in their riot helmets. If anyone attacks you, take their goddamn guns and use them... If you attack us today, by the power of our God, we'll mop the goddamn streets with you, the goddamn bastards."

These are among the nicer things Khalid has said about whites over the years. Khalid Muhammad's hatred of whites is so vociferous and lacking in subtlety that it is a wonder why he continues to live in such an oppressive society — or is it?

Born Harold Moore Vann, he served three months in a Georgia prison in 1987 and was on parole for two years. He claims to have a PhD from Dillard University, although Dillard says he attended classes but never got a degree. Likewise, he claims to have taught African studies at California State University at Long Beach, but California State has never heard of him.

What he *has* done which can be verified is make a ton of money spouting anti-white diatribes to suckers who have made him a millionaire. In 1993, as a spokesman for the Nation of Islam, he received $2,650 for a speech at Kean College in Union, New Jersey, where he advocated that South African blacks give whites 24 hours to leave and kill any who stayed behind. "We kill the women. We kill the babies. We kill the blind. We kill the cripples. We kill them all... When you get through killing them all, go to the goddamn graveyard and dig up the grave and kill them a-goddamn-gain because they didn't die hard enough."

When he praised the Long Island Railroad mass murderer Colin Ferguson before a New York City crowd of 25,000 blacks, he received a long ovation. On the Phil Donahue Show, Khalid asserted that Nelson Mandela was a front man for white supremacists. More recently, he told a gathering at San Francisco State University to "use violence when necessary" and added, "I want to see a movie that shows us killing white folks so hard the blood is flowing into the popcorn." Admission to this event was $7.00 for students, $10.00 general admission, and $15.00 for "racists."

The Nation of Islam has long been preaching the extermination of whites. This is actually quite a normal conclusion for a movement which believes whites are devils who were created in a laboratory by a mad black scientist named Yacub about 6,000 years ago on the Isle of Patmos.

There can be only one cure then, both simple and obvious, for what ails Khalid Muhammad—voluntary repatriation to Africa. As an American citizen, Khalid Muhammad is free to live wherever he wants in the world (assuming that country will have him.) Why on earth would he choose to continue to live in a polity where he is a part of a racial minority which, by his own admission, is oppressed by a bestial majority? Why does Khalid Muhammad, with his vast wealth, continue to make his home in a country where 74 percent of the population are devils?

Actions, of course, speak louder than words. Even in everyday life, more is known about people by how they lead their lives, where they make their homes and with whom they choose to associate than by what they *say*. This is not to suggest that Khalid Muhammad doesn't really hate whites, simply that he is too smart to hate them enough to abandon the infrastructure of a successful society which only whites could have built.

Just as white liberals spend their lives preaching about the importance of integration and multiculturalism, yet choose to live themselves in white neighborhoods, so also do Khalid Muhammad and other anti-white black radicals, despite their rantings, demonstrate through their actions the desire to live in an "oppressive" society where they enjoy a standard of living incalculably higher than the one they would encounter in the Dark Continent. They may wear African garb and choose African names, but Khalid and his followers have also chosen running water, electricity and modern technology over principle and the backward society that goes with it.

In fact, in Khalid Muhammad's case, the desire to exterminate whites would have to begin not with the majority in general, but with his own neighbors. He lives in a luxury apartment building in Cliffside Park, New Jersey in which he is the only black person. His building has an olympic-sized swimming pool and tennis courts to go with the Rolls Royce and Mercedes that he drives. Oppression is tough in America.

But taking Khalid at his word, the only cure for what ails him is choosing one of the 44 nations in sub-Saharan Africa to make his home. He would never again be a racial minority and would not live in a devil-dominated society which he claims is the source of all the world's evils. Oh, and per capita income is roughly $200 per year.

2
AFFIRMATIVE ACTION

The Real "Discrimination"

Discrimination against white people — otherwise known as affirmative action, set-asides, preferences and racial quotas — is enjoying its last gasp. But just as a vampire does not die without a silver bullet or a stake through the heart, proponents of the affirmative action monster will not accept death easily.

Bill Lann Lee, nominated by President Clinton for the nation's top civil rights post, is the embodiment of racial radicalism. Lee, longtime lawyer for the contemptible NAACP, is so committed to racial quotas that he favors overturning California's Proposition 209, which outlawed state-sponsored racial and gender preferences. Prop 209 was passed by the voters of California in 1996 and it abolished all government affirmative action programs. In a landmark victory for fairness and common sense, qualifications and merit would prevail without regard to race.

A dictator disguised as a federal judge, with the enthusiastic support of the Clinton Justice Department, then trampled on the will of California voters and blocked implementation of Prop 209, ruling it unconstitutional on the bizarre grounds that by mandating that all people be treated equally, minorities will therefore be treated unequally.

In April, the 9th U.S. Court of Appeals upheld Prop 209, dismissing the dictator's nonsensical decision. Two weeks ago, the Supreme Court refused to hear further discussion on the case, thereby handing California voters a major victory, the Clinton Administration a well-deserved defeat, and white people a fair chance. The path presumably has been cleared for the rest of the country to follow suit. Rest in peace, affirmative action.

Now, Bill Lann Lee, fighting for Senate approval, reaffirmed his opposition to Prop 209 before the Judiciary Committee. Republican Chairman Orrin Hatch was horrified by Lee's testimony, which hinted strongly that he would be more than soft on racial quotas, despite his sworn obligation to enforce the law. With this, Lee's chances of confirmation appear to have gone up in smoke.

In response to Lee's pending defeat, putrid liberal Senator Patrick Leahy called Lee — in a transparent touch of irony — a "superb Asian-American," implying that opposition to Lee was essentially the result of more racism. In 1997, accusations of bigotry remain the last refuge of a scoundrel. The original limousine liberal, Ted Kennedy, chimed in that "the party of Lincoln should not be the anti-civil rights party." Only in the strange world of American political jargon could the term "civil rights" stand for special treatment for non-whites. (Lincoln, incidentally, was opposed to today's version of "civil rights," but that's a detail.)

But despite these promising successes, many spineless whites who are clearly intimidated by the likes of Jesse Jackson and NAACP President Kweisi Mfume, have demonstrated a shameful timidity on the issue. Rather than take advantage of the momentum (and follow their own professed principles), these shallow folks have backed down and given the vampire a stay of execution.

For example, the House of Representatives was set to pass legislation ending all federal affirmative action programs. At the eleventh hour, they delayed action indefinitely. Republican Congressman George Gekas said, "Rushing headlong into the issue without building a national consensus will only be seen as political and divisive."

What? If not for immense voter support on this "divisive" issue, the Republicans would never have taken control of the House in the first place.

The early results are in and they are profound. With race no longer a consideration, black and Hispanic applications for university admissions in California are down 7.7 and 5.8 percent respectively. And this is only in anticipation of the changes, which do not go into effect until next year. White enrollment, on the other hand, is up 10.4 percent.

The problem with affirmative action — in addition to its inherent unfairness — is that it will never produce true equality *in results*. Standards for admissions and hiring must be artificially lowered in order for non-whites to gain positions which they are otherwise not entitled to. Examples abound, but one of the most horrible examples is the case of Patrick Chavis, a black man who was permitted to enter medical school over more qualified whites, thanks to the infamous Bakke decision of the Supreme Court in 1978. This June, Chavis was suspended by the California Medical Board for his "inability to perform some of the most basic duties required of a physician." He has been sued 21 times for malpractice.

The national trend is finally giving whites the equal treatment they want and which proper justice demands. The cowardly sheep who are allowing affirmative action to continue, albeit on a respirator, should lead by example and give up their own jobs to an "underprivileged" non-white.

Laws of Lunacy

When the Civil Rights Act of 1964 was passed, it was to have ushered in a new era. A brave new America would emerge where employers could no longer discriminate against persons on account of race. Because of government enforcement of this fair and color-blind mandate, blacks, no longer held back by discrimination, would eventually attain at the same accomplishment level as whites.

Then a strange thing happened on the way to utopia. It didn't work. Since there continued to be a discernible gap in white/black test scores, job-related abilities and overall accomplishments, the civil rights laws were turned on their heads. Though they strictly *forbade* discrimination by race, they came to *require* discrimination by race — against whites. In the name of non-discrimination, the law overtly practices discrimination. The flawed logic behind this upside down application was that if the races were not achieving equally, it must be due to yet more pervasive white racism.

Since this was the logic that guided the law, there existed an inherent contradiction within the law because equality of *opportunity* would never actually produce what the social engineers really wanted: equality of *results*.

The two, of course, can never exist at the same time — with a perfectly level playing field different races will excel in different areas. So the civil rights laws, which claimed to be race-neutral, necessarily came to be interpreted as requiring discrimination against whites. Affirmative action, racial preferences and set-asides became the law of the land. Employers, therefore, are breaking the law if they discriminate and are also breaking the law if they *do not.*

Most Americans think it is wrong to discriminate on account of race, but they also believe that all people should be treated fairly, not given special preference. The original objections to the civil rights laws were both theoretical and constitutional. The original intent of the Tenth Amendment and an honest reading of it clearly allows the states to pass laws without interference from the federal government. As a theoretical and libertarian matter, the anti-discrimination laws took away precious freedoms — the freedom for employers to choose who they want as employees. For the first time in American history it became a crime for a businessman to simply choose not to conduct business — not hiring a person he didn't want.

It is as a practical matter, however, that anti-discrimination laws — from the original 1964 Act to the more recent Civil Rights Act of 1991 — have degenerated to an advanced state of lunacy. Laws which purport to "level the playing field" and assure fairness actually run roughshod over the very concept of equal opportunity. The grotesque evolution of anti-discrimination laws were at first caused by court decisions but were then formalized as law by the federal government, especially after Reagan appointees began reversing the trend.

The laws that govern employment decisions made every day in the United States are predicated on the assumption that employers spend most of their time scheming how to avoid hiring competent blacks. Since it has been virtually impossible to find companies that actually do thus discriminate, "racial discrimination" lawsuits are now brought strictly on the basis of numbers. Individual blacks who can show no proof that they were discriminated against, sue simply because the number of blacks hired by the offending company does not match blacks in the surrounding geographical location.

Often, deliberate discrimination is *not even claimed* in these suits. The charge is usually "unintentional" discrimination with racism the "probable" reason, although no one can quite find it. With the laws set up this way, companies wishing to avoid expensive lawsuits simply hire by the numbers and are saddled with less qualified non-whites, while turning qualified whites away. If they don't do this, they will be found to have broken the law.

In 1991, Northwest Airlines was faced with just such a lawsuit. After exhaustive expenditures, the company finally gave up and agreed to spend $3.5 million to accelerate the hiring of blacks. Northwest admitted no discrimination and none was proven. But the terms of the settlement required that they do discriminate — against whites. In 1996, Texaco chose the same way out. Sears Roebuck took the more principled but expensive path. It spent $20 million over 15 years to get a verdict of innocent and save its good name. But the message is clear: companies are smarter to simply hire by quota and pay ransom rather than defend expensive lawsuits.

Likewise, because of anti-discrimination laws, men and women must pay the same rates for life insurance even though women live longer. Actuaries not needed. Because of the Americans with Disabilities Act, AIDS is now considered a "handicap" and an employer cannot refuse health insurance to someone certain to run up high medical bills. Only the American government can legislate such unjust madness in the name of justice for all.

"Disparate Impact" and Race-norming

The creation of anti-discrimination laws has led to some of the most bizarre and gruesome concepts ever articulated in the history of employment practices. These mutations — built up through court decisions and formalized by law — are all the more ridiculous due to the fact that their birth was predicated on the idea of equality. But the obsession of social engineers with equal representation by race has necessarily led to discriminatory practices in the name of anti-discrimination. Because race-neutral policies were not resulting in an equal number of black doctors, lawyers, engineering students, police sergeants and sanitation workers, "anti-discrimination" laws had to be adjusted to specifically recognize race, notwithstanding that the original rationale behind these laws was to *ignore* race.

Due to inconvenient results by race, job standards and requirements became subject to the absurd doctrine of "disparate impact," which was first invented by courts in the early 1970's and written into law in the early 1990's.

If an employer, for example, is hiring clerks to be responsible for some paperwork, answering phones and billing, and requires that applicants for the jobs have a high school diploma, and then chooses from the pool of interested people without regard to race, he is guilty of racial discrimination. How? Whites are more likely than blacks to have high school diplomas, so requiring a diploma has a "disparate impact" on blacks. Obviously, the concept of "disparate impact" does nothing but wither away even the most minimal standards and forces employers to accept a less-qualified workforce.

The 1991 Civil Rights Act mandates that only the rock-bottom qualifications for a job be required. The standards must be "job related" and have a "business necessity," both very ambiguous terms. Needless to say, no reasonable person believes that requiring a high school diploma is discriminatory. But anti-discrimination laws are rarely reasonable.

Blacks, of course, are generally less qualified than whites by almost any standard, so by the reasoning of "disparate impact," virtually any requirement is deemed discriminatory. What should be seen as an attempt by employers to maintain the highest standards is looked upon as racial discrimination in the insane world of anti-discrimination laws.

There was a time when police and fire departments turned away applicants who had been dishonorably discharged from the military. Since blacks receive twice as many dishonorable discharges as whites, the practice is said to have a "disparate impact" and is no longer allowed. A legal manual for fire departments explains that the EEOC has ruled that "arrest records cannot be used to disqualify applicants, as experience shows blacks are arrested substantially more frequently than whites in proportion to their numbers."

Can all this be for real?

To combat the problem of "disparate impact" on job test scores (since whites outscore blacks on every test ever invented), the concept of "race-norming" was introduced. In 1981, the U.S. Department of Labor established this new method of scoring the General Aptitude Test Battery (GATB), a standardized test of general ability which had been used since 1947 to evaluate applicants for a wide range of jobs. The basic thrust of race-norming is to compare a person's score not against those of all other applicants, but against *only those of people belonging to the same race.* Thus, blacks would be compared only to blacks, whites to whites, etc.

Say, for example, that a white, an Asian, a black and a Hispanic all scored 300 on the test. By "race-norming" the scores, blacks would be placed in the 87th percentile — very high; Hispanics in the 74th percentile; and whites and Asians near the bottom, in the 47th percentile. This resulted in perfect racial symmetry and guaranteed the racially balanced workforce that utopians wanted, to hell with standards.

According to these results, blacks indeed *were* in the 87th percentile — but only judged against other blacks. So jobs went to extremely less-deserving blacks instead of whites or Asians. Whites would have to essentially score double the black scores to get the job. And the social engineers responsible for this travesty define "race-norming" as fair.

Before whites found out about race-norming and it was banned in 1991, some 16 million Americans had their scores adjusted by this method, most of whom were never told. By 1986, 40 state governments and many huge corporations like Nabisco and Anheuser-Busch were given race-normed candidates by state agencies, without being informed that their workforce was severely below standard.

"Race-norming" was finally made illegal because of the bad

publicity attending it. But Congress did not ban using the doctrine of "disparate impact," which "race-norming" was supposed to cure. So the current law is a contradiction within itself. "Disparate impact" can now legally only be cured by companies simply hiring by racial quota, only without the trouble of standardized tests.

Is this fair?

That Elusive "Test Bias"

Since fact is usually more ludicrous than fiction, there are times when it is beneficial for the fragile human condition to simply enjoy the hilarious side of things in order to keep one's sanity. For if a reasonable person were to expect justice in egalitarian America, he would lose his mind examining the government's desperate search to find "cultural bias" on standardized employment tests.

It is axiomatic that blacks never score as high as whites on standardized tests. Though every heroic effort has been made to see that they do, the gap in average test scores remains wide — and constant. Some of the most well-publicized cases of differing test scores have been on those given by police departments for promotions to sergeant or captain. Since it is a violation of orthodoxy to attribute the differences to inherent ability, "cultural bias" in the tests has been declared the official explanation, even though no one can ever find it. But just as Alfred Hitchcock would say of his movies that the fun was more in the chase itself than in actually finding the culprit, so it is with the perennial hunt for that elusive test bias.

It is perplexing to imagine exactly what kind of "cultural bias" could possibly sneak into a written examination given to people who are already professional police officers, but such logic never stands in the way of the search. The New York City Police Department battled lawsuits for ten years which claimed that its test for sergeant was biased against blacks and Puerto Ricans, since the test results dictated that 95 percent of the promotions would go to whites. The department took the extraordinary step of inviting the most vocal minority critics of the test to help design the new "bias-free" test. All were satisfied until the smoke cleared and the test scores came in exactly the same. Since it would have been rather awkward for these same critics to continue to claim that the test was biased, they instead claimed the "results" were biased. The department was hit with another lawsuit.

When it began to dawn on everyone that minorities would simply never pass any test that required reading and writing at the same rate as whites, the police decided to replace the written exam with a video-taped exam. Again, all was peaceful until the results proved, sure enough, that the *video* must have been biased!

San Francisco police likewise spent nearly $1 million over a five-year period trying to devise a test that non-whites could pass at the same rate as whites. When the expected results came in on the "bias-free" test, a judge ordered that 22 minorities be promoted over whites who scored higher.

But perhaps the most hilarious example of this exercise to exorcise "bias" from tests was the innovative approach taken by the Houston Fire Department. With court approval, the department set out to eliminate bias *after the fact*. A 100-question exam for promotions was given, with 70 being the passing grade. Naturally, whites got the highest scores. The department then hired an independent consulting firm to examine the results and determine which specific questions minorities were more likely to get wrong than whites. Those questions were to be thrown out on the rationale that if minorities got them wrong, they "must have been" biased, even though no one could figure out why.

Sure enough, the consulting firm eliminated 28 questions deemed biased against minorities, meaning 32 people who had originally passed, now failed: 24 whites, four blacks, three Hispanics and one Asian. 13 who originally failed, now passed: five blacks, four Hispanics and four whites. The end result was that eight minorities were knocked off the pass list, but nine were added, so this entire endeavor concluded in a net gain of one minority.

Naturally, those knocked off the pass list, including the minorities, were furious. But the funnier aspect of this lunacy was that it was a piece of tough luck on those blacks who got the *right* answers on those questions that were supposed to be biased *against them.* And it was a stroke of great luck for those whites who got the *wrong* answers to questions that were supposedly biased *in their favor.*

The federal government, of course, has also participated in a variety of silly crusades to eliminate "cultural bias" from tests. When the Federal Service Entrance Examination was in wide use in the 1970's, blacks could simply never pass it at the same rate as whites, notwithstanding that they were given extra points just for being black. Amidst great fanfare and at significant expense, the government designed a new test, the Professional and Administrative Career Examination (PACE), which it swore would be free of bias.

Oops. 42 percent of whites passed, while 13 percent of Hispanics and only 5 percent of blacks did. PACE, naturally, had to be scrapped. The feds, essentially throwing their arms in the air, gave up testing altogether, and instituted a system of hiring interviews and evaluations which made it easy to hire minorities without the embarrassment of having to point to low test scores. A federal judge ruled this process "arbitrary and capricious," but minorities were being hired so it continued to be used.

This entire comedy routine of eliminating "test bias" is the result of anti-discrimination policy executed in the alleged interest of "fairness," "justice," and "equal opportunity."

3
IMMIGRATION

Damn Lies and Immigration Myths

Although immigration is generally considered a "controversial" or "hot-button" issue, there is really no reason why it should be. There are very few issues on which Americans are in such agreement. Over the past four decades, and especially since the disastrous Immigration Act of 1965 which opened America's floodgates to a new brand of third world aliens, never more than 13 percent of the American people have wanted increased levels of immigration. Since immigration has quadrupled in that time, there has never been a more clear case of American politicians defying the will of the people they are supposed to be representing.

So immigration is "controversial" only because ululating radical groups and elitist legislators and members of the intelligentsia have thumbed their noses at the American people, not because there is any true divisiveness of opinion on the matter. There is also no other issue about which so many myths exist. The definition of a Big Lie is that when an untruth is repeated often enough and with little or no refutation, it becomes a truth in the minds of the people. It is astounding how the immigration myths are believed and spouted by even many otherwise informed and intelligent people, on both sides of the political and ideological spectrum.

As a matter of basic philosophy (without considering its pragmatic effects), immigration is often thought to be a human right, or a "civil right," in today's jargon. The reality, of course, is that *no one* has the "right" to come here, any more than a person has the "right" to enter someone's home. Immigration is, in fact, a privilege granted by, and at the complete whim of, the American people through their elected representatives. It is only in practice that legislators ignore the people's wishes. So a foreigner is neither being wronged nor violated when he is prevented by American laws from entering the United States.

Moreover, the American people are under no legal or moral

obligation to come up with any particular justification for restricting immigration. As a sovereign nation, the United States can forbid immigration for any or no reason.

Nevertheless, any discussion of immigration cannot proceed for very long without someone mouthing the famous mantra, "We are a nation of immigrants." Although not a myth in the literal sense, these words are certainly a myth in the spirit in which they are meant. The impression is that somehow America has always been unique in that its citizens are comprised of those who migrated here or whose ancestors did. The fact is that *all* nations are "nations of immigrants." In other countries, did people simply sprout out of the ground? What has made America unique is the *rapidity* with which immigrants formed the country. Rather than hundreds or thousands of years, the American immigration experiment occurred in mere decades.

The myth of America's historical immigration policies holds that the United States has always permitted large-scale immigration from all corners of the globe. This revisionist version of history maintains that relatively open borders have allowed foreigners to enter without regard to race or culture, and basically anyone could be an American since America was based on a set of ideas, not a particular race or ethnicity. All of this is patently false.

The history of American immigration has always included severe restrictions, both in the way of "who" could enter and when. It is *because of these restrictions* that the immigration experiment worked so well (at least until 1965, when the influx of third world aliens was let loose.)

The very first naturalization law, enacted in 1790, required that applicants for American citizenship be "free white persons." It is pure nonsense to suggest that it was America's intention to include people from all over the world. Until the effects of the 1965 Act began driving America to ruin, the United States was a self-consciously white nation and it was *deliberately* so. Laws were passed in the late 19th century which essentially barred Asian immigration. The "Great Restriction" Quota Act of 1921 was purposely enacted to prevent immigration — through a system of national origins quotas — from anywhere other than Europe, in order to reflect America's existing ethnic and racial heritage.

Contrary to popular belief, the United States had always halted immigration substantially after periods of great influx. These pauses for "digestion" were enacted in order to allow for the proper assimilation — "Americanization" — of immigrants. And remember, this was done for *European* immigrants, those most easily assimilable.

Today's immigration enthusiasts are among the most blatant historical liars. If the true history of American immigration were still followed, the United States would not be the alien nation it has become.

Immigration: Social & Economic Calamity

At the turn of the century, during what is called the "First Great Wave" of immigration, 40 percent of arriving immigrants eventually returned home. With no safety net, European newcomers sank or swam based on their own abilities to succeed in America. Today, during the "Second Great Wave" (which is 90 percent non-European), we have the welfare state — and no one leaves.

Earlier immigration policies required that no immigrant become a "public charge," a financial burden to the United States. Skills and the ability to support oneself were paramount. Now, because of the worst piece of legislation in American history, the Immigration Act of 1965, the American nation will never be as it once was. A greater percentage of immigrants are on welfare than native-born Americans. Last year, $20 billion more in welfare payments were given to aliens than they paid back in taxes. Currently, immigrants comprise 25 percent of the prisoners in federal penitentiaries, and the number is rising. In 1997, Washington politicians made a "budget deal" which scaled back $115 billion in Medicare services to American senior citizens, partly to pay for supplemental income assistance for aliens. And all this includes *illegal* aliens. Break American laws and receive a cash reward for life.

How pathetic is this American loss of will? When an illegal alien, claiming the earned income tax credit, is detected through his fake social security number, *the IRS assigns him a temporary number and mails the check anyway!* As Peter Brimelow remarks in his book *Alien Nation*, "Got to get that check in the mail!" Fully 83 percent of illegal aliens have false social security numbers, but confidentiality laws forbid reporting them to the Immigration and Naturalization Service. Break an American law and you will be protected by an American law.

Today's aliens—legal or illegal—are profoundly less skilled, less educated, more crime-prone, far less inclined to assimilate, and are an economic and social albatross. They are neither expected nor required to learn English. Cast your first vote with a foreign language election ballot! Despite the stories of penniless immigrants arriving and becoming valedictorians and nuclear physicists, it is far more likely that they will wind up on welfare or in prison.

Contrary to what immigration enthusiasts say, there is no evidence whatsoever that today's immigrants are "revitalizing" cities. That is more of a rhetorical political statement than a factual one. Never have Americans been given so much of what they have overwhelmingly and consistently made clear that they do not want. The ridiculous interpretation of the fourteenth amendment, "birthright citizenship," means that aliens illegally cross the border and give birth five minutes later. The child is automatically an American citizen. The parents become citizens due to "family reunification" policy, and on and on and on.

These open borders, which have resulted in 2 to 3 million illegals a year, have left the United States open to many diseases previously thought to be extinct. Tuberculosis, non-existent by the 1970's, is back with a vengeance, thanks to aliens from Latin America, where the disease is widespread. Leprosy, measles, cholera, malaria and a strain of yellow fever are among the gifts American immigration policy has brought.

INS officials admitted recently in Congressional testimony that they granted citizenship last year to 18,000 aliens with criminal records. This spineless capitulation knows no bounds. The United States solves its illegal immigration problem by simply granting "amnesty" to illegals. "You were illegal — now you're legal!" Break American laws and get mass clemency. The illegals who continue to cross American borders have every reason to expect another amnesty.

Remarkably, some of the tough laws, such as the "public charge" and English proficiency statutes are still on the books. They are simply never enforced. Immigration laws work only against those few who choose to obey them. In Hong Kong and Taiwan, there is a best-selling book which advises would-be immigrants on how to qualify for the American Social Security Income program upon arrival in the United States. Latin American and other third world countries offer the same instructions. It should come as no surprise, therefore, that better than one in five immigrant households receives some form of taxpayer largess — more than double the native-born white rate. In addition, Congress has made it illegal for prospective employers to favor citizens over non-citizens.

American handouts are so tempting that aliens have no shame. A dark-skinned Egyptian is suing the federal government to have his racial classification changed from white to black, in order to qualify for affirmative action programs.

The world is laughing at the United States. And our "leaders" fiddle, while America burns.

Alien Nation

Catastrophic immigration policies are transforming the United States beyond recognition. The Census Bureau has projected that if current immigration and non-white birth rates continue, European-Americans will be a minority — below 50 percent of the population

— within a few decades. Just 30 years ago, America was still almost 90 percent white. Today, whites are 74 percent of the population, and falling.

The coming demographic calamity is something we are told to anticipate with great joy. The declining dominance and influence of America's European core is said to be a wonderful thing. If it does indeed come to pass, there are already ample signs which demonstrate what it will really mean: the American nation, as it has existed for over 200 years, will no longer be.

According to Peter Brimelow, "There is no precedent for a sovereign country undergoing such a rapid and radical transformation of its ethnic character in the entire history of the world... History suggests little reason to suppose it will succeed." In fact, there is every reason to know it will fail. The invasion overtaking the United States is so alien to anything previously thought to be "American," that the dissolution of America is the only possible outcome if current trends continue.

What happens when one nation invades and conquers another? History shows that certain things always occur. The conquerors impose and expand their way of life — culture, language, habits, and the entire fabric of the old country — on the conquered territory. Refugees are always created of the conquered people. They either flee or live under the domination of the conquerors. For all intents and purposes, the old country is re-created in the newly-won territory.

Say, for example, Mexico were to invade and conquer the southern parts of Texas and California. What would they do? They would expel much of the white population and replace it with Mexicans. American holidays like the Fourth of July would be ignored and Mexican ones like Cinco de Mayo would be celebrated. Mexican flags would now adorn store fronts and homes. Spanish would be spoken by everyone instead of English. Election ballots and government forms would be printed in Spanish and stores would sell only Spanish-language newspapers and magazines. Music, food, work and leisure habits would all become Mexican. Now conquered, this American territory would become Mexico re-created.

Guess what? *This is exactly what has already happened.* The greatest and most powerful nation in the history of the world is losing, without a single shot being fired and without any resistance, what nations have always fought to the death to preserve.

Aliens have invaded and taken over parts of the United States which remain American in name only. Jared Taylor writes, "Most people who grew up in America, want to grow old in America, not in some bustling outpost of Mexico or Southeast Asia." Referring to the massive white flight which has taken place because of the invasion, he continues, "Americans should not have to move to Montana or Idaho to grow old with people like themselves." Of course, if current immigration policies continue, there will be no refuge in Idaho or Montana either. This demographic shift of white American "refugees" proves what everyone knows: aliens create cities in which whites cannot and will not live.

Multiculturalists and other anti-Americans do not attempt to hide their glee. Arnold Torres of the League of United Latin American Communities, says, "We cannot assimilate and we won't. We will bury you." Groups like Movimiento Estudiantil Chicano de Aztlan are using American tax dollars to carve out parts of the American Southwest to be reunited with Mexico. Parts of New York and every major city are essentially part of Latin America now. Forever lost to Western civilization.

People rarely think of the end of civilizations because, in the scheme of things, the process is very gradual. But throughout history, the greatest of civilizations have perished. If examined carefully, it is not difficult to see what America's fate will be.

Brimelow describes the situation, "We've all seen a speeded-up film of the cloudscape. What appears to the naked eye to be a panorama of almost immobile grandeur writhes into wild life. Vast patterns of soaring, swooping movement are suddenly discernable. Great towering cumulonimbus formations boil up out of nowhere, dominating the sky in a way that would be terrifying if it were not in real life so gradual that we are barely aware that anything is going on."

But the clouds also melt away. Just as the American nation will melt away if the treasonous capitulation by the United States government is allowed to continue, snuffing out what is historically the brief American moment, like a momentary flame in the wind.

Last Gasp of White America?

America-haters and other third world degenerates were dancing in the streets last week when a federal judge threw out Proposition 187, the California initiative that would have cut off state-funded benefits for illegal aliens. By obliterating the will — by a landslide — of California voters, Judge Marianna Pfaelzer's tyrannical ruling will have ramifications that will dwarf in importance the fallout of last week's more famous ruling — the dismissal of the Paula Jones suit. Only the Supreme Court can save Prop 187 now.

In 1994, when the referendum was gaining steam, Prop 187's detractors pulled out all the stops in an orgy of anti-Americanism that made national news. Unlike congressional votes, where alien partisans can depend upon the cowardice of politicians, Prop 187 (like the anti-affirmative action Prop 209) was a direct vote of the people. It was, therefore, guaranteed to pass.

In a pre-vote protest rally, tens of thousands of welfare-bred aliens brandishing Mexican and Guatemalan flags shouted, "Viva la Raza!" (Long live the Race.) "This Proposition 187 is a Declaration of War against the Latino/Chicano community in this country," said one speaker. A leader of the communist Brown Berets threatened in a newspaper editorial, "The streets will run red with blood of tyrants who have murdered us for so long."

The notion that illegal squatters should be entitled to the benefits of American tax dollars and welfare is something only the mind of a dictator judge could postulate. And these leaches are not Americans, not in fact and not in spirit. This Chicano movement is based on a concept called "irredentism," which means the reclaiming of land thought to be one's own. Not only is their no intention of assimilating into American society, the movement considers itself a separate nation. The territory to be reclaimed for Mexico includes California, Nevada, Utah, Colorado, Arizona, New Mexico and Texas. Their name for this territory is "Aztlan," which means "the brown continent."

Through mass immigration, legal or illegal, it is the goal of these revolutionaries to return Hispanic domination to the land area of "Aztlan" and they are not shy about saying so. Ricardo Chavira, writing in *Time* magazine, stated, "Imagine the ludicrousness of an elementary school teacher telling a room full of Chicanos that George Washington and company were our Founding Fathers. Obviously, those guys in matching white wigs were no fathers of mine."

American taxpayers, those complacent suckers, pay for public university newspapers that support the alien conquest of the United States. In *La Voz Mestiza*, a Chicano student newspaper published at the University of California-Irvine, staff writer Timoteo Curichiche told Americans in an expletive-filled tirade, "The sulfuric cauldrons of Hell await you. And if it's up to us to send you there; then so be it. Let's settle the score. You've spilled enough of our blood, now it's your turn to bleed you [expletive] subhuman beasts."

Another tax-funded newspaper, *Voz Fronteriza*, wrote, "It must be laid out to our people that the struggle is not about being 'part of the gringo colonial system' but one for the complete liberation of our Raza and the reunification of Aztlan and Mexico." A flyer put out by the National Chicano Moratorium Committee declared that "Proposition 187 has been brought on by an increasingly fascist gringo AmeriKKKa which is terrified by a growing Chicano Mexicano population and a wave of Raza nationalism which is sweeping over Aztlan-Mexico Ocupado (that region which the gringo falsely names the 'Southwest U.S.')."

Certainly, the silent majority of decent Americans cannot say they haven't been warned. Yet radical aliens must look on in astonishment as, time after time, white Americans behave like passive sheep in the face of their own dispossession. "La Raza" could only be so brazen while so outnumbered when secure in the knowledge that whites seem to operate with a death wish, sitting idly by while their country is taken from them. What do anti-Americans think when they see American judges make rulings which—if taken to their logical conclusion — would dissolve the republic?

These are the glorious results of the multiculturalism that whites are constantly brow-beaten into "celebrating." This is the "cultural enrichment" that the American people are told is such a wonderful thing. This is the "diversity" that is supposed to be such a great source of strength.

The spirit of Proposition 187 should be replicated by every state as the salvation of the American nation. But with leftist judges overruling democratic decisions and a cocky opposition, the struggle remains daunting.

Addressing a conference of radicals, former California State Senator Art Torres declared confidently, "Remember, Proposition 187 was the last gasp of White America..."

We'll see.

4

POLITICS AND GOVERNMENT

Bogus Charges of Bank Bigotry

Congressman Chuck Schumer has made a splash recently with his well-publicized report that purports to show that New York City banks practice "race bias" regarding home mortgage applications. The Schumer report, which claims to have uncovered "wide spread" racism, states that blacks and Hispanics are "twice as likely" as whites to be rejected for mortgages, even when they have the same or greater income than whites. Although the report analyzes 48,000 home mortgage applications in the five boroughs of New York City, Schumer suspects that such bias exists "throughout the country."

As with practically all charges of racism in contemporary America, a close examination of the facts and the details reveals a far different story. The charge that minorities are "twice as likely" to be rejected, although technically correct (assuming the report is accurate), is very deceiving and is far less dramatic than it appears. Numbers can be reported in such a way as to make them say whatever the analyst wants them to say. For example, Schumer's own report concedes that blacks are approved at an overwhelming rate. But rather than say they are approved 77.4 percent of the time, the report says they are "rejected" at a 22.6 percent clip (thus "twice" the white rate of 11.1 percent.) Suddenly, when it is reported that whites are approved 88.9 percent of the time, Hispanics 81.8 percent and blacks 77.4 percent, the differences do not seem all that great.

In a letter to bank presidents, Schumer acknowledges that other factors such as credit history and asset levels are part of the consideration when deciding on applicants, but finds it "difficult to believe that these secondary requirements are so vastly different between minority and white applicants." Of course, if the numbers are examined honestly, those factors need not be so vastly different to account for the rate of rejection differences.

Susan Weeks, spokeswoman for Schumer's biggest target, Citibank, explains that many factors can account for the eleven point difference in black and white approval rates, even if income is identical. Calling Schumer's charges "erroneous," Mrs. Weeks says, "We consider many things when deciding whether or not to approve a mortgage application — how long a person has lived at current residence, history of paying utility bills, length of time at current job, income versus current debt, and overall stability. These things can certainly explain the difference." If anything, Citibank could more accurately be accused of bending over backwards for minorities. They target non-white areas with special programs, seminars, and direct mail and work with neighborhood housing services to show people the easiest way to obtain a mortgage.

Needless to say, it is a very peculiar form of "racism" which approves black applications more than three-quarters of the time.

Schumer would be holding a trump card in his hand if he could show a difference in default rates. Indeed, if banks were practicing bigotry and holding blacks and Hispanics to a higher standard of credit worthiness, by definition these applicants would have lower default rates than the whites who were approved for mortgages while being less qualified. Alas, no such smoking gun exists.

In the same vein, it has often been claimed that the Scholastic Aptitude Tests are biased against minorities, despite all evidence showing that the SAT test scores accurately measure college performance. If the tests were biased, then blacks, naturally, would outperform whites with the same scores. The evidence shows that they do not, thus obliterating the "bias" argument.

On a more common sense level, banks, like all corporations, are very hard-headed about profits and are in business to make money. It is a preposterous notion that bank executives deliberately deprive themselves of profits by withholding loans to credit-worthy blacks in order to indulge in racism. Even the Jim Crow laws down South, which legislated blacks out of certain jobs, were an implicit admission that Southern businessmen could not be trusted to discriminate against blacks if such racism hurt profits.

There are really only two definitions of "racism" as it applies to the American social and political scene. A "racist" is, in the first place, anyone winning an argument with a liberal. "Racism," according to the second definition which more closely applies to those poor banks targeted in the Schumer report, is any *result* that "professional" minority activists and their partisans don't like. These reflexive charges of bank bigotry seem, as always, to place the burden of proof on the accused, where no real evidence of guilt exists.

Reparations Madness

There was a hilarious skit from the old British comedy Monty Python's Flying Circus, in which a roomful of well-bred tuxedoed gentlemen are sitting around an oblong table when the meeting of the Society For Putting Things On Top Of Other Things is called to order. The chairman asks for a report from the Brighton Branch of the Society. The representative from Brighton stands to report that the members of the Brighton Branch have been very successful of late in putting things on top of other things. The room erupts in thunderous applause.

The chairman then calls upon the representative from Liverpool who proudly states that the Liverpool members have, too, been very successful in putting things on top of other things. More applause.

Finally, the chairman calls for an update from London. John Cleese then stands, an apprehensive and apologetic look on his face, when he tells the Society, "Frankly, the members in London think the whole thing's quite silly."

And so it is when something so ridiculous is actually proposed by serious people with a straight face. Now that Bill Clinton and a host of loonies are proposing an official apology for slavery -- and the inevitable demands for reparations, more affirmative action, ad nauseum that go with it -- one almost expects John Cleese to stand up and reveal the whole thing as a gag.

This constant state of atonement that America finds itself in can be attacked on several levels. This most recent call for an official public government apology for the institution of slavery is part of

Clinton's larger National Discussion of Race. If the American nation deserves any public statement on the issue, the statement should be one of congratulations -- the United States is the only nation to end slavery of its own volition. Likewise, it is the only nation to come up with moral justifications against slavery while it was still in place. Furthermore, America pushed the rest of the world to abandon the practice, and history shows that if not for the moral impetus of the West, slavery would have continued widespread throughout the world.

But let us examine Clinton's arguments on the details and the merits. First, there is the absurd notion that descendants of wrongdoers owe the descendants of those wronged. Guilt by Generation. This peculiar logic, even if adhered to, is not consistent or specific. It basically means that the whites of today must apologize to and compensate the blacks of today. But is it limited to only those descendants of those who can be proven to have been slaveholders? And only those who are descended from slaves? What about Italian, Irish and Jewish Americans whose families came here at the turn of the century -- thirty years after slavery ended? Are they exempt from the apology? Is their tax money exempted from the reparations? What about the descendents of those blacks never enslaved? What about black slave owners? What about descendants of white slaves? (Yes, there were white slaves.)

Once all this is sorted out, we can address the issue of compensating and apologizing to someone who was never himself wronged. The call for the apology and reparations is exactly the way affirmative action operates. Special treatment based on race, regardless of whether personal injury can be shown.

The whole notion is so preposterous that only intelligent people could have thought it up. When the Japanese interned in the camps during World War II were compensated, it was those personally wronged who were compensated, not descendants or people of the same race. But the apology and reparations enthusiasts do not care much for logic. They intend to push white guilt to the limit. And, unfortunately, it is not only white liberals this time. Even Newt Gingrich has hinted that an apology is in order. Thankfully, some brave black voices of sanity -- Ward Connerly and Thomas Sowell most notably -- have called the apology a ridiculous idea.

Jesse Jackson, of course, says that an apology is only a first step. Reparations, more social programs and affirmative action are also necessary.

What about a white demand for black gratitude for all the well-intentioned programs that have already failed? Yeah, right.

The details of the world history of slavery and slavery in the United States are not simple matters. That blacks were enslaved is not in dispute. But most of the important details are conveniently overlooked or misrepresented.

Black slavery in the United States is usually presented as uniquely evil in the annals of human bondage. But Europeans and Americans almost never went on slave-hunting excursions into the middle of Africa. Long-established African slave traders wanting to sell off surpluses sold to white Americans. So most slaves were already slaves, having been enslaved by other blacks.

Most of these were captured in tribal wars, where the custom was to enslave captured women and children but to kill all the men. Thus, if not for the demand for slavery in the New World, these men would have been slaughtered.

While there was an abolition movement in the United States, those who held slaves often developed an affection for them and treated them rather well, at least in comparison with slavery throughout time. While there was certainly cases of brutality, they were exceptions. In *The Mind of the South*, W.J. Cash writes that "no one but a cur beat, starved, or overdrove his slaves became a living rule of daily conduct; a standard so binding as to generate contempt for whoever violated it."

According to Clarence Carson in his *History of the United States*, slaves often spent much of their day in activities of leisure, while current history texts focus only on beatings. Some studies show that by certain measures slaves fared better than free blacks. For example, the slave infant mortality rate was 153 per thousand. As late as 1915, the infant mortality rate among blacks in Massachusetts was 163 per thousand, 185 in Pennsylvania and 192 in New

York.

Although it is politically incorrect to say so, there is no question that the descendants of black American slaves are among the luckiest people of all time. If not for past slavery, they would have remained in the Dark Continent, where today they would be enjoying no running water, no electricity, a banana republic economy, mass starvation, illiteracy and all the other joys that go with living in black Africa.

In the United States, thanks to a white infrastructure, blacks enjoy a standard of living way out of proportion to what they would be experiencing in black countries.

Black radical Congressmen John Conyers and Walter Fauntroy were actually two of the first serious people to speak of reparations in modern times. In 1989, Conyers introduced legislation that would, he said, create the first federally chartered commission to study the impact of slavery and of "subsequent and continuing discrimination against African-Americans, and make recommendations to Congress on whether some remedy should be made to the descendants of slaves."

Louis Farrakhan's version would include the release of all black convicts! Also a militant organization called the "Provisional Government of the Republic of New Africa" is demanding that Congress grant blacks resettlement land in five southern states -- South Carolina, Georgia, Alabama, Mississippi and Louisiana -- which they would run as a separate nation.

Kwame Afo, the Vice President of the "Provisional Government", said that the cost to compensate blacks for slavery would be $4.1 trillion! This calculation (there are others) is based on individual compensation for every American black!

According to Human Events, "The notion of reparations for every black who is descended from slaves seems so ridiculous on its face that the initial reaction of many is to dismiss it out of hand. But it is clear that Conyers, Fauntroy, and the network of black activists whom they are working with across the country intend to make reparations into a cause celebre."

The largest and best known group demanding compensation

for a practice that ended 130 years ago is the National Coalition of Blacks for Reparations in America (N'COBRA.) Vince Goodwin, the group's chairman, says slavery is "the largest holocaust committed."

Unbelievably, even a white neo-conservative, Charles Krauthammer, favors reparations as an alternative to affirmative action. Dorothy Lewis of the Black Reparations Committee explains that this will not do. "Affirmative action is needed to curtail racism that exists *now*."

Other calculations are so hilarious that it is difficult to report them in what is intended to be a serious essay. Andrew Jenkins, a Detroit real estate agent and long-time reparations activist, says that every black in the country is entitled to $1 million. According to William Robertson Boggs, "It does not seem to bother him that this would work out to about $30 trillion, or the equivalent of the entire federal budget for the past 20 or so years."

There are more modest versions, with the stingiest being Krauthammer's, which would give $100,000 for every black family of four.

Reparations enthusiasts maintain that the government promised freed slaves 40 acres and a mule and that this gives today's blacks a legal claim. Even ignoring for a moment the issue of those never wronged being compensated, the fact is that the government never "promised" any such thing. It was Thaddeus Stevens who proposed such legislation and his bill never became law. It was more his intention, moreover, to humiliate the Southern aristocracy than to benefit blacks.

Some of today's loonies want to figure the worth of 40 acres and a mule in 1865, and then add the accumulated interest to the present. This comes to $98,191.35 per black person.

There is also the nonsensical claim that the United States became prosperous because of the labor of blacks and, therefore, their descendants are owed. First of all, there exists a large body of evidence that slavery was not even profitable. Those parts of the country where slavery was most common were always and remain still the poorest. Eugene Genovese, a Marxist historian adamantly opposed to slavery, argued in his writings that slavery actually retarded the development of the South. He argued that since slaves could not be taught to handle livestock, the South did not develop a cattle industry.

Only in cotton fields was slavery profitable. Frederick Law Olmstead, the architect who designed New York's famed Central Park, estimated in his study that on many Southern plantations, slaves worked only one third as much as a hired hand on a New England farm. What most Americans do not realize is that due to the excessive leisure under slavery, many Northern abolitionists actually argued against slavery on the grounds that the nation's productivity would rise if blacks were freed and became subject to Northern employment practices.

All of this, of course, is pure madness. There is no legal basis for rewarding and punishing the living for acts committed by people who are dead.

A more sensible question is will American whites be compensated for the loss of jobs and promotions because of government-sponsored affirmative action programs?

Bill Clinton's constant breast-beating on the issue of race is vintage 1990's America. If he feels guilty, let him apologize as an individual. Leave the rest of us alone. Or bring out Monty Python's John Cleese.

The National Endowment for Pornography

The Republican-controlled House of Representatives is on the verge of breaking one of its most solemn promises. If indeed House Republicans renege on their vow to permanently exterminate the National Endowment for the Arts, the result may well be political suicide and a return to Democratic control. It will be a death well-deserved.

The taxpayers of the United States first became aware that their money was being spent on child pornography, "homoerotic" art and various other assortments of squalid filth and blasphemy when the National Endowment for the Arts scandal erupted several years ago.

It was during the Bush Administration that the NEA thrived under the leadership of George Bush's hand-picked chairman, John Frohnmayer, who brazenly declared, "I will not be the decency czar." The most well-known examples of taxpayer-funded obscenities were the sadomasochistic photographs of radical AIDS-infected homosexual Robert Mapplethorpe. Other works of "art" were "Piss Christ," by Andres Serrano which depicted a crucifix in a vat of urine. The Mapplethorpe gems included photos of a man urinating into the mouth of another, a leering man with a nine-foot bullwhip trailing from his rectum, and two photos of nude children in suggestive poses. For the first time in American history, something funded and officially sanctioned by the United States government was the subject of an obscenity trial which took place in Cincinnati, because their display violated community standards.

In September of 1995, House Majority Leader Dick Armey asserted, "The NEA shall cease to exist in two years. So long as I am majority leader, I will not schedule an NEA authorization bill for floor consideration that would violate our agreement of a two-year, $99 million per year phaseout."

Well, Dick Armey is still majority leader, more powerful than he was two and a half years ago, and not only is the NEA still alive, but the House is in the process of authorizing yet another $100 million.

The "art" which the American people are forced to subsidize includes the NEA-funded "play" of Karen Finley, where she casually peels off her dress and pours gelatin into her bra, slathers chocolate on herself, sticks blobs of bean sprouts all over her body and calls it sperm. This "art" was banned in London and threatened with vice squad response in Los Angeles. The "Annie Sprinkle" performance featured public urination on stage. Kedric Wolfe, a recipient of NEA funds, showed up at a press conference in support of a colleague whose similar obscenity performance was banned. He arrived nearly naked, wearing only a skimpy loincloth made from two American flags.

A $20,000 grant for a stage act called "Machine Performance" held in Lewiston, New York featured the burning of Bibles onstage. A poster advertising the "play" asked for public Bible donations. It contained doctored photos of nude white men being burned on stakes, which surround a Bible with a pitchfork piercing its cover. In the show, large sexually explicit props were covered with a generous layer of requisitioned Bibles. After employing these props in a wide variety of unholy rituals, machines burned them to ashes. The poster advises, "Bibles can always be obtained for free from hotels, churches... and your parents' houses. Be advised that in certain instances theft is a moral obligation."

A $15,000 grant was awarded to avowed lesbian "performance artist" Holly Hughes and collaborator Ellen Sebastian for "No Trace of the Blonde," a stage act described in the grant proposal itself as "concerned with gothic imagery of vampirism, the suppression and anxiety surrounding female sexuality... The work will be created for up to five performers with two pubescent girls, black and white, about twelve years old, the main characters." *U.S. News & World Report* described Hughes as "a playwright who wants to advance lesbianism and whose performance onstage includes a scene in which she places her hand up her vagina, saying that she saw 'Jesus between Mother's hips.'"

An NEA film produced by the San Francisco International Lesbian and Gay Film Festival, "Tongues Untied," was refused air time by more than 200 PBS affiliates nationwide because of its vulgar obscenity and graphic homosexual nudity scenes. A similarly grotesque film called "Poison" contained graphic scenes of seething homoeroticism, homosexual intercourse and many other lewd, profane and violent acts. Frohnmayer said he would stake his reputation on its artistic merit.

Frohnmayer was finally fired when Pat Buchanan challenged Bush in the presidential primaries and began running television commercials of scantily clad, dancing homosexuals which Bush was funding. (At first, Bush had the nerve to call the commercials "obscene.") Thankfully, Frohnmayer's head is on Pat Buchanan's mantelpiece.

Now, the Republicans must decide if they will keep their promise and protect the American taxpayer from funding the NEA's pornographic filth... or be tossed out on Election Day on their bullwhips.

Statehood for Puerto Rico?

The United States of America is on the verge of adding Puerto Rico to the Union as the 51st State.

If such a calamity should take place, what the nation will really be getting is a third world basket case and a welfare-addicted albatross. If the current bill before Congress culminates in statehood, Puerto Rico would immediately become the country's poorest state, easily surpassing the current poorest, Mississippi, by a mile. In 1995, Puerto Rico's per capita income was $7,670 — *less than half* that of Mississippi.

In Puerto Rico, food stamps are so widely used that they are basically a second currency. Prostitutes accept them as payment. The Puerto Rican rates for AIDS, drug abuse, crime, poverty, illegitimacy, and unemployment are astronomical. Wonderful news for the American taxpayer who will be forced to subsidize this annexation. Its current AIDS rate would place Puerto Rico third in the nation (after New York and Washington, D.C.); the drug addiction rate of 1,972 per thousand dwarfs the current United States rate; the murder rate in Puerto Rico is two and a half times that of the U.S.; and unemployment on the "welfare capital of the Caribbean" is 20 percent — compared to 5 percent for the United States.

It is no mystery why the Democrats are pushing so hard for Puerto Rican statehood. It will guarantee two more Democratic members of the Senate and six more Democrats in the House of Representatives. Needless to say, all these Puerto Rican Democrats will further the cause of domestic welfarism, of which Puerto Ricans will participate in at an inordinate rate. A report from the General Accounting Office indicates that were Puerto Rico a state, it would receive an additional three to four *billion* dollars from Washington, while paying only $49 million in income taxes. According to Puerto Rico's congressional delegate Carlos Romero-Barcelo, the island's contribution to the federal treasury would be far less than any other state in the Union. Per capita benefits, on the other hand, would be greater than any state. Clearly, the only incentive for statehood on the part of Puerto Ricans is financial, not loyalty to the United States or a patriotic desire to be Americans.

From 1898 to 1952, the United States ruled Puerto Rico as a territory with an appointed governor following the American invasion during the Spanish-American War. In 1952, Congress made it a self-governing commonwealth, whereby Puerto Rico pays no federal income tax and cannot vote in U.S. elections, but can travel freely and receive some handouts. Statehood would break open the bank and new demands for cultural accommodation would undoubtedly follow.

Puerto Rico is an island of four million Spanish-speaking non-whites, of which only 16 percent consider themselves American. Only 20 percent of Puerto Ricans speak English. Puerto Rico is culturally alien to the United States and Puerto Ricans see themselves as members of a distinct Latino-Caribbean culture, totally incompatible with the Anglo-American tradition. They are right. Ruben Berrios Martinez of the Puerto Rican Independence Party writes, "Puerto Rico's heart is not American. It is Puerto Rican. The national sentiment of Puerto Ricans is entirely devoted to our *patria*, as we call our homeland in Spanish, our language. We are Puerto Ricans in the same way that Mexicans are Mexicans and Japanese are Japanese. For us, 'we the people' means we Puerto Ricans."

Indeed, making Puerto Rico a state is akin to making Mexico or Nigeria a state. Puerto Ricans field their own teams during the Olympics (and cheer loudest when their teams face the United States) and participate independently in international beauty pageants. Even pro-statehood Puerto Ricans do not pretend that loyalty to

America or cultural kinship and affinity with the United States are their motivations. All prominent spokesmen for statehood emphasize the financial windfall and nothing else. Many even go out of their way to make this point, so as to not alienate Puerto Rican nationalists. Puerto Rico is so addicted to welfare that author Robert Fernandez notes that some aid centers in the capitol city of San Juan handle more "clients" than the entire state of Texas.

Like a bunch of giddy lemmings, Republicans are also supporting the bill as a misguided way of courting Hispanic voters. The strategy, of course, will fail as the Republicans march cheerfully to their position of permanent minority status.

Where do Americans stand in all this? What say do American citizens actually have in whether or not to allow an alien nation into their sovereign union, which will inevitably cause them such cultural strife and economic hardship? What authority do Americans have in deciding if an island of aliens, who do not even consider themselves Americans, should be made a part of the United States? Not very much. The way the bill works, only Puerto Ricans will hold a plebiscite to decide if they want statehood, independence or retain commonwealth status.

Puerto Ricans have the right to choose their own destiny, and the island should be given its independence. But only Americans should retain the authority to approve the admittance of a new state, and whether they want to subject their nation to such a cultural and economic catastrophe.

A "Sorry" Excuse For a President

Bill Clinton has finally apologized. Not to Paula, Kathleen or Gennifer — but to Africa. Proving once again that he is not too big to grovel at the feet of dictators, nor above confessing to all sins except his own, America's First Apologist has said he is sorry on behalf of the United States, in whose name he claims to speak.

Clinton actually set the precedent for this Official Regret last year when he foolishly apologized to American blacks for slavery. Now, in his prance around Africa, the President is blaming the United States for everything, including the weather. "European Americans received the fruits of the slave trade, and we were wrong in that," he said.

The *New York Times* headline blared, "In Uganda, Clinton Expresses Regret on Slavery in U.S." Uganda is a very curious place to apologize for slavery. Firstly, no American slaves came from Uganda. But more importantly, Clinton's own State Department has reported that today in Uganda "school age children" are abducted regularly by rebels "for sale as slaves, or for sexual purposes."

Moreover, the man standing next to Clinton when he made these remarks, Yoweri Museveni, the "President" of Uganda, is the leader of a one-party military regime who came to power by way of a "fraudulent" election, according to the State Department. The Ugandan government, which is typical of regimes in sub-Saharan Africa, expressly limits freedom of assembly and association. But even Museveni showed more sense than Clinton on the issue of slavery when he remarked, "...if anyone should apologize, it should be the African chiefs."

Ever the gracious guest, Clinton conspicuously neglected to speak about *today's* slavery, not only in Uganda but in other parts of Africa as well. In the Sudan, the cases of slavery, servitude, forced labor and the slave trade have increased dramatically. The State Department reports, "women and children were sold and sent to the north or abroad to work as domestic servants, agricultural laborers, and sometimes concubines." Given the opportunity to do so, Clinton has refused to impose sanctions on the government of Sudan.

Clinton's gush of remorse did not end with slavery. He also apologized to the Dark Continent for United States conduct during the Cold War, when American presidents were forced to align with anti-communist polities in order to contain Soviet expansion. If ever the American government was united and consistent on any matter, it was during the protracted conflict against worldwide revolutionary communism led by the Soviet Union. Notwithstanding their other shortcomings, four liberals (Truman, Kennedy, Johnson and Hubert Humphrey) courageously stood up against communism. After forty years of containment, Ronald Reagan finally won the Cold War for the West.

Having spent some of his college years in Moscow protesting the United States, Clinton, a '60's flower child, has not forgotten whose side he was on. "The United States has not always done the right thing by Africa," he said. "In our own time, during the Cold War... we dealt with countries in Africa and other parts of the world more on how they stood in the struggle between the United States and the Soviet Union than how they stood in the struggle for their own people's aspirations to live up to the fullest of their God-given abilities."

Having established himself as the moral superior to his predecessors, the President concluded, "Perhaps the worst sin America ever committed about Africa was the sin of neglect and ignorance."

It is, of course, *his own* ignorance that was revealed during Clinton's African excursion. The United States owes no apologies to Africa. Africans have indeed lived in miserable and desperate conditions. But these were brought about by their own incompetence and backwardness. Black Africans have shown themselves to be utterly incapable of building modern economies. Since European colonialism ended in the last 30 years, leaving Africans in charge of their own nations, starvation and disease have risen sharply, and lawless barbarism between rival tribes has cost millions of lives.

African dictators routinely raid their countries' treasuries while their own people starve. Western aid has poured into the Dark Continent by the billions, only to be stolen and squandered by ruthless pirates who show no evidence of concern for the African people. Yet Bill Clinton, standing with the perpetrators of these acts, apologizes for and blames the United States.

Humility and forgiveness, it is said, are part of being Christian. Billy Graham (the preacher, not the wrestler) says he forgives Bill Clinton's sexual sins — a peculiar "forgiveness" since Clinton denies having committed these sins. Nevertheless, the President has shown a remarkable propensity to apologize — never for his own transgressions, but for the fabricated wrongs of God's Country.

UN: Get Lost Already

The United Nations, that cesspool of squalid tinpot dictatorships, undertook to investigate the United States several months ago for possible human rights violations. This is not a misprint. Yes, the *U.N.* investigated the *U.S.* on human rights, which is on the order of the World Wrestling Federation investigating St. Patrick's Cathedral for crude behavior.

The U.N., whose members include such bastions of freedom and civil liberties as Iraq, Iran, Cuba and Uganda, believes it has the moral authority to pass judgement on America, whose citizens continue to pay for one-fourth of the U.N. budget. The chief investigator, someone named Bacre Waly Ndiaye, a citizen of Senegal, was described as "a U.N. Human Rights Commission specialist on extrajudicial, summary and arbitrary executions" when this comedy routine began in November. Today, newspapers are referring to him as the U.N.'s "Special Rapporteur," which probably means he is also a rap singer.

Well, the verdict is finally in and indeed, according to the report just released by Rapper Ndiaye, the United States is guilty of "racism" and violating "international law" in administration of the death penalty. The report, thankfully, will not be taken seriously by the usually guilt-ridden American government. When this farce commenced, Ndiaye was not well-received by American prison authorities, and even the Clinton administration was surprisingly uncooperative. Senator Jesse Helms called it "an absurd U.N. charade."

Nevertheless, Ndiaye spent months roaming American prisons, interviewing murderers. At one point he said death sentences in America resulted from legal proceedings "which fall short of international guarantees for a fair trial." Of course, the "international guarantees" one would find in most U.N.-member countries' prisons would be tortured, starving, "re-educated" citizens fortunate enough to not have been shot for criticizing their government. Now, the report states "imposition of death sentences in the United States seems to continue to be marked by arbitrariness. Race, ethnic origin and economic status appear to be key determinants of who will, and who will not, receive a sentence of death."

The report actually endorsed legislation already rejected by the United States Congress, the "Racial Justice Act" of 1994, which would have effectively eliminated the death penalty by applying strict racial quotas to the condemned — a sort of lethal injection by affirmative action. Since blacks commit most murders, capital punishment could never be applied in a manner which would satisfy the racial bean counters.

In the report's concluding theory, where the leopard finally reveals his spots, the U.N. actually *blames democracy* for America's supposedly poor record on human rights. "It is difficult to determine the influence that the electorate and a financial contribution to an election campaign may have on a judge," says the report. "It is certain that this situation exposes the judge to a higher level of pressure than those who, like federal judges, hold life tenures, do not have to run for reelection and are not accountable to volatile public opinion." In other words, civil liberties are better protected by dictatorships and totalitarian regimes since despots need not worry about elections and "volatile public opinion."

The important point regarding this amusing United Nations sideshow is not so much the nonsensical absurdities of the accusations, but the creeping acquiescence of the United States to U.N. authority. This gradual surrender of American sovereignty to the high priests of world government has already manifested itself in the loss of American life. Al Gore has praised American soldiers for giving their lives "to the United Nations." American foreign policy, more and more, has become beholden to U.N. resolutions and the word of the Security Council. If officials from criminal regimes can inspect American prisons, what will be next? Will American citizens be subject to the judgements of U.N. rather than U.S. courts?

Right now, the United Nations claims that the United States owes "back dues" and the Clinton administration foolishly agrees, charging the Congress with making America the world's biggest "deadbeat nation." The United States already squanders tens of billions of dollars on this putrid organization, not to mention endangering American lives in "peacekeeping" missions.

American taxpayers should refuse to pay these "dues" and the next Bacre Waly Ndiaye should be denied admission to American institutions. In fact, United States membership should be discontinued and the entire U.N. monstrosity booted from midtown Manhattan to some third world outpost, where it belongs. Besides, aren't the Yankees searching for a new location for the Stadium?

The Road to World Government

For citizens of the United States, the road to world government is an incremental one. But it is no less stark and real. Although loss of American sovereignty can only occur gradually, the threat is no longer latent and the forces are already in motion. Most of the engines which will subordinate Americans to foreign powers and international institutions are firmly in place, encroaching on American freedoms, and violating the Constitution.

"I'll bet that within the next hundred years... nationhood as we know it will be obsolete; all states will recognize a single, global authority. A phrase briefly fashionable in the mid-20th Century — 'citizen of the world' — will have assumed real meaning by the end of the 21st."

The person who wrote these words is not some New Age kook in a remote neo-socialist university. Rather, they were written by Strobe Talbott, appointed deputy secretary of state by Bill Clinton, making him the nation's highest ranking diplomat behind only the

Secretary of State and Clinton himself. The significance of Talbott's assurance of the inevitable ascendancy of world government is not only that he is such a high-ranking United States official with considerable authority, but that his statement was one of *advocacy* for world government, not a warning. Talbott has spent his entire career pushing for the dissolution of the American nation and the destruction of American sovereignty.

Talbott continued, "Meanwhile, the free world formed multilateral financial institutions that depend on member states' willingness to give up a degree of sovereignty. The International Monetary Fund can virtually dictate fiscal policies, even including how much tax a government should levy on its citizens. The General Agreement on Tariffs and Trade regulates how much duty a nation can charge on imports. These organizations can be seen as the protoministries of trade, finance and development for a united world."

Indeed, the International Monetary Fund, one of the "protoministries" Talbott is so fond of, has increased its power substantially due to the efforts of the Clinton Administration. When American taxpayers bailed out the defaulting Mexican government to the tune of $20 billion, Clinton persuaded the IMF to pledge another $17.8 billion, 18 percent of which is yet more American money.

After the bailout, Clinton moved to institutionalize the IMF as a permanent mechanism, with authority over member nations. This means the IMF can order American taxpayers to cough up more money, *without the approval of the Congress and without even the safeguard of a United States veto.* The IMF, regulated by no one, has forced Americans more recently to bail out Thailand, Indonesia and the Philippines.

Another "protoministry," the World Trade Organization, can now subordinate American laws — both federal and state — to its own dictates. When Clinton signed the WTO charter, the organization came to possess the authority to supersede United States sovereignty on all matters relating to trade and commerce.

Article 1, Sections 8 and 10 of the Constitution give Congress the exclusive power "to lay and collect... duties" and "regulate commerce with foreign nations..." With the WTO now able to shred the Constitution at its whim, Newt Gingrich admitted "we are transferring substantial power to an international body that can coerce us to change our behavior." In the WTO, the United States has only one of 117 votes, with each member nation having equal power. And there is no U.S. veto.

Even some liberals are alarmed. Harvard Law Professor Laurence Tribe testified that the WTO's power will trample on the states' Tenth Amendment rights to make their own laws without interference. When the WTO ruled that the United States must change its Clean Air Act because it hindered the ability of Venezuela and Brazil to import their oil, the Clinton administration agreed to honor the ruling — without the permission of Congress and the American people.

The complete surrender of sovereignty has seeped into other areas such as criminal justice. The Clinton Administration has endorsed the idea of an International Criminal Court which would have the power to try Americans before foreign judges and juries coming from countries which do not recognize the basic civil rights which protect Americans under the Constitution. Most nations involved in the drafting of such a court do not, for example, support the concept expressed in the Fourth Amendment, protecting citizens against unreasonable searches and seizures. *Human Events* asks, "Which way would a Pakistani vote?" if Norman Schwarzkopf were accused of bombing a civilian target.

In supporting these dangerous institutions which subordinate Americans to foreign rule and surrender U.S. sovereignty to third world control, Bill Clinton has violated his oath of office in which he swore to "preserve, protect and defend the Constitution of the United States." That his own appointees explicitly support such a surrender to world government can only be regarded as an act of treason.

Impeach Him For Treason, Not Sex

Although Bill Clinton has now committed perjury for the second time in eight months, not much will change. Having lied to the grand jury in January and then forcefully and emphatically told the American people several weeks later that he did not have a sexual relationship with "that woman," he has finally admitted to perjury without actually admitting it — all in vintage Clinton style. His supporters will continue to defend him, even when that dress is proved to have been decorated with his DNA. Many will continue to keep a straight face when they say they believe him. And those who are honest enough to concede his crimes will still say it's "only about sex."

In due time, the name Henry Hyde, the Illinois congressman who will oversee any impeachment proceedings, will become as much a household name in America as Monica's. Indeed, if the issue was only sex, Clinton should not lose the job he was elected to, notwithstanding that even if the Lewinsky affair had never happened, Bill Clinton has still proven to be the most dishonorable man to have ever occupied the White House. But while the American press has been consumed with Monica-mania, Clinton has quietly sold out the nation's security in a development so astounding as to almost defy reality, even for him.

In the early 1950's, at the conclusion of the most sensational congressional hearings of this century, Alger Hiss, the high-ranking State Department official, was convicted of perjury for lying about his role as an agent for the Soviet Union. The damage done by Hiss' transfer of secrets to America's sworn enemy was incalculable. But suppose President Truman had knowingly handed over to Stalin secrets that would imperil national security. Ridiculous? Yes... for Truman.

What most Americans are unaware of, essentially due to non-coverage by major media, is that Bill Clinton has given communist

China the necessary technology it needs to effectively launch missiles carrying weapons of mass destruction to United States targets. In April, *Human Events* reported, "The President's latest sellout to China would be unbelievable did we not already know Bill Clinton so well... Thanks to Bill Clinton, China is now better able to vaporize your hometown than it was a year ago... Had this been done by anybody other than the President under full color of law, it would have been viewed as a criminal act of treachery."

China has already threatened to use its weapons against the United States, but did not possess the accuracy in its guidance systems needed for a successful launch before being given a helping hand by the President. Officially, the United States government had in place export-control restrictions on this sophisticated technology to China for obvious security reasons. Two American firms, Loral Space & Communications and Hughes Electronics had lobbied the administration for five years to lift the restrictions. These companies found it much cheaper to launch their satellites in China than in America but Chinese rockets lacked the necessary technology and American restrictions prohibited China from getting it.

As it turns out, both Loral and Hughes are heavy contributors to the Democratic Party. Loral CEO Bernard Schwartz was, in fact, the Democrats' largest single contributor in 1997. Hughes CEO Michael Armstrong was soon named chairman of the President's Export Council, in a blatant conflict of interest. Both men continued to push Clinton hard to shift the regulatory authority from the State Department to Ron Brown's Commerce Department, which Clinton finally did in 1996. (The State Department is primarily concerned with national security; Commerce with profits.) A "civilian" satellite which Clinton permitted to be launched in China promptly exploded in a residential neighborhood.

Scientists from both Loral and Hughes then gave the Chinese, according to the *New York Times*, "200 pages of data, analysis evaluation and reports" to help them correct the problem. When the State Department investigated this illegal transfer of technology, the Pentagon report concluded that "United States national security has been harmed." A federal grand jury was convened to probe Hughes and Loral.

Incredibly, with the grand jury investigation still ongoing and with his own State Department bemoaning the damage done to American national security, Clinton signed a waiver to the export-control laws in February allowing another satellite launch in China and another technology transfer. Clinton's own Justice Department opposed the transfer since it would undermine its grand jury investigation of Hughes and Loral, but he signed the waiver anyway.

Of course, it is entirely possible that Bill Clinton is simply stupid. But that is unlikely since he approved the transfer of technology *after* he was informed by the Pentagon that the move would be harmful to national security. Moreover, unlike Jimmy Carter and George Bush, Clinton's worst transgressions have always involved matters where he knew full well what he was doing. If giving crucial technology to an adversary nation that will more easily enable the destruction of American cities is not an act of treason, what is?

5
CRIME AND GUN CONTROL

The Unjust Saga of Bernhard Goetz

In April of last year, in a civil courthouse in the Bronx, the unjust saga of Bernhard Goetz finally came to a close. New York's subway gunman, having endured twelve grueling years which included a criminal trial, eight months in prison, worldwide publicity and civil lawsuits brought by the men he shot, was told by a jury of non-whites to pay $43 million to the wheelchair-bound Darrell Cabey, one of the four black hoodlums who tried to rob him.

In order to fully understand how this calamity came to be, it is necessary to go back in time and rediscover just how the Bernhard Goetz affair unfolded and ultimately what it all means...

Exactly ten years ago this month, across the street from the Bernhard Goetz criminal trial, in a different courthouse in downtown Manhattan, two black hoodlums were on trial for viciously slashing the face of New York fashion model Marla Hanson in a premeditated attack the summer before. There was little question as to the guilt of the perpetrators, prompting the defense attorney -- black racial hustler Alton Maddox of Tawana Brawley fame who has since been disbarred -- to resort to the underhanded tactic of "putting the victim on trial."

This tactic, commonplace in cases of rape, is distinguished by attacks on the credibility and attitudes of the victim in order to demonstrate that she "asked for it." In the Hanson case, since both defendants were black, Maddox proceeded to tarnish the beautiful model's testimony, referring to her as a "Texas girl" with "racial hang-ups." Hanson and her attorney publicly expressed their outrage at this despicable tactic and, after the guilty verdict was delivered, Judge Henry Atlas blasted Hanson for "criticizing actions in my courtroom in the media," bringing Hanson to tears.

A public outcry followed, and petitions were circulated outside the courthouse calling for Atlas' resignation. Two days later, Atlas apologized to Hanson in a televised news conference, claiming he now understood her outrage at being "the victim on trial."

While all of this was transpiring, something similar, but not precisely the same, was going on at the trial of Bernhard Goetz. Indeed, my sense of decency was offended by the events at the Hanson trial. But the ultimate travesty of justice was occurring at the Goetz trial, where the victim was *literally* on trial.

Welcome to the Twilight Zone. By now the script and cast are well-known: on December 22, 1984, Bernhard Goetz, a white electronics expert, boarded a New York City subway car on a Saturday afternoon to meet some friends downtown. Soon after entering the train, Goetz was surrounded by four black criminals -- all with long records and histories of violence -- in a menacing and intimidating manner, demanding money from him. Indeed, based on their collective histories, extortion was the most innocent of their intentions. For the Gang of Four, just another day at the office. Goetz, who three years prior had been brutally beaten by a street criminal, decided he would not be a victim again.

After his previous encounter with violence, Goetz applied for a pistol carry license. Denied by New York's prohibitionist gun control laws, even after appeals and thousands of dollars of lawyers fees, Goetz decided to carry an unlicensed weapon for self-protection. Armed with this pistol for three years without incident, Goetz now realized it could save his life.

As the four moved in on the trapped Goetz, he opened fire -- "the shots heard 'round the world!" -- nailing all of them, and the only noise louder than the shots themselves was the sound of cheering New Yorkers.

After the shots were fired, Goetz became a fugitive and an instant celebrity. Passengers on the train were so terrified of the four assailants and so supportive of Goetz' actions, that when the police arrived on the scene in search of the unknown gunman, these passengers sent them in the *wrong direction.*

Finally surrendering to police two weeks later, Goetz was the recipient of an unprecedented show of affection from average citizens and an equally profound attack by the political establishment. For two and a half years he was a political football, persecuted by the gutless Manhattan District Attorney Robert Morgenthau (who still holds the job), who went after Goetz with a sinister passion, in order to please the radical element of the screwed-up New York establishment, which Goetz' attorney, Barry Slotnick, termed "the fringe radicals."

In January 1985 (one month after the shooting), a grand jury acquitted Goetz of all but minor gun charges. In an unprecedented maneuver -- clearly in response to radical black political pressure from the likes of Al Sharpton -- Morgenthau proceeded with a fury and convened a second grand jury. He claimed to have what he termed "two secret champagne witnesses", who in reality turned out to be two of the hoodlums who attacked Goetz. Their bogus testimony was used to indict Goetz on attempted murder and assault charges. Self-defense against criminals was taboo in the city of Koch and Morgenthau.

In condemning Goetz, the bleeding hearts have always argued against Goetz' decision to fire by stating that he could not have known that the four had criminal records. This is a most curious argument. Of course, it was precisely because Goetz had never met the four that more credibility is attached to his actions. Had Goetz been acquainted with the previous activities of the four, he would have been more prone to overreact to their mere presence.

Of course, the same apologists who claim that the records of the predators were not known by Goetz and, therefore, are irrelevant in this case, are the same ones who, had the four been choir boys, would have wept, "See, that proves they were not intending to rob him."

The nature, character, and backgrounds of the Gang of Four were not disputable. In fact, all but the wheel-chair bound Darrell Cabey committed crimes *after* the shooting.

"The People vs. Bernhard Goetz", as this trial was so offensively christened, had scores of witnesses and exhibits, but not much of a prosecution case. Nine days after the shooting, Goetz made an audiotape confession to police in New Hampshire, where he had surrendered and, later in the day, made a videotaped confession to New York police who had traveled there. Both tapes, each roughly two hours in length, were played before a mesmerized courtroom.

The contents of the tapes were analyzed, reanalyzed and much-ballyhooed in the press after their showing in court.

On the tapes, a clearly distraught Goetz editorialized on every subject from the court system, to the school system, to the crime situation. At one point he stated, "The legal system is a sham. I'm not hiding a thing. I'm not gonna hide behind this idiotic legal system. The legal system is a joke. It doesn't serve the people. It's a self-serving bureaucracy. It gives the whole legal profession, all the attorneys, jobs and this and that. The more screwed up it is, the more jobs people have."

Goetz also showed a disdain for legal technicalities which have nothing to do with morality. "New York has never been concerned with right and wrong. It's concerned with the paperwork, the formalities, the technicalities. I'm just sick of it."

Ironically, Goetz would see so much of these technicalities at his very own trial two and a half years later. I had never attended a trial in its entirety before the Goetz criminal trial ten years ago. If I went into it with distrust, I came out with disgust. The entire debacle was one of silly rulings and technicalities, with no consideration whatsoever for morality. It was like a baseball game where one roots for his team in a partisan manner and hopes for favorable calls from the umpire, regardless of whether or not the umpire is actually correct in his ruling.

An example of this was when the prosecutor, Assistant District Attorney Gregory Waples objected to a Slotnick question to hoodlum Troy Canty, the first one to approach Goetz and demand money. "At the time of the shooting, you were a bad person," Slotnick stated.

"I object!" Waples yelled.

The question was permitted, but I cannot comprehend why any sane person would object to Canty being called a bad person. After all, prior to the shooting, Canty was guilty of being a drug addict, robbing video machines, assaulting young girls and old ladies, shoplifting, beating up a teacher, and stealing money intended for handicapped children. How insulting to Mr. Canty to be asked if he was a "bad person."

In the nine years between the criminal trial and last year's civil trial, Canty managed to enter a drug rehabilitation program at one point instead of prison as part of his deal with Morgenthau for his testimony. He was, however, eventually arrested for robbery again.

At the time, the pro-criminal element was falling all over itself justifying these technicalities which routinely free violent criminals. The stock defense was generally as follows: "What people have to understand is that these technicalities are a necessary evil. They exist so that when the occasion arises when a truly innocent person is accused, they have full protection. Freeing obviously guilty criminals is sometimes necessary to protect *your* rights."

This all sounds great, and some parts of it may have constitutional validity, but the sentiments were always expressed by anti-Goetz liberals as justification for apologizing for the criminal behavior of the four assailants. Somehow, decent people have always felt their rights were better protected if criminals did *not* get off on technicalities. The right to life and to walk the streets safely for example.

But try and use this very same reasoning regarding the Second Amendment in support of Bernhard Goetz and those with this technical mentality will run for cover. Since they usually favor tight gun control, they oppose citizens carrying guns on the grounds that "a normally decent citizen may go crazy if he gets his hands on a gun."

On talk shows at the time, I attempted to use the same argument: "To risk the fact that an otherwise decent citizen may recklessly fire a gun (though there is no evidence that this happens at any discernible rate) is a necessary evil if we are to protect all citizens' rights under the Constitution to keep and bear arms. Tolerating such unfortunate incidents is necessary to protect *your* right of self-defense."

Michele Kern, a St. John's University law student and spectator at the trial, not surprisingly possessed this mentality. Describing herself as "basically pro-Goetz", she sympathized with Goetz' plight and recognized the nature of the predators, but had reservations about decent citizens carrying firearms.

"The city would be unsafe if it became easy to carry a gun. People carrying guns would tend to create a more violent society," she said. "It is alright to defend yourself, but you should do it within your means."

Wonderful. So Bernhard Goetz should reasonably have expected to defend himself against four violent thugs within his means. What means? Unfortunately, Miss Kern's statement accurately reflects New York City's nonsensical law. Basically, the law states that one has the right to use deadly force if one reasonably believes he is about to be robbed. But the *right to possess* the means to employ such force is against the law. You have the right to *use* a gun lawfully for self-defense, but you do not have the right to *own* or *possess* the gun.

The Goetz criminal trial was, of course, a mutant, a freak of nature. If morality, rather than legality, was truly the issue, there would have been no case against Bernhard Goetz. (There was not much of a legal case, either.) The district attorney's case was one of technicalities. He could have avoided the robbery by merely showing the gun, they claimed. Were the final three shots justified? Were the perpetrators running away after the first shot? Did Goetz exceed the limits of proper response?

Judging strictly the pragmatic effects of his actions, Goetz provided a tremendous service to citizens who take to the streets and subways in fear. For an entire month he eliminated the criminal activities of three hoodlums, and permanently ended the life of crime of the crippled Darrell Cabey. Goetz exposed the laughingstock criminal justice system as it had never been exposed before and opened the door for an expression of moral health by supportive New Yorkers.

Then-Mayor Ed Koch ordered thirteen hundred police out to find Goetz when he was on the run. Real violent criminals need not have worried about such a man-hunt in New York. Defending this extraordinary number of police at the time of the shooting, Koch proclaimed, "We will not tolerate vigilantism." He also claimed Goetz' actions rose from "the same animal baseness that gave rise to the Holocaust." That same week, then-Governor Mario Cuomo described Goetz's actions as "dangerous and wrong." There were, of course, no actions which subway riders feared *less* than those of Bernhard Goetz.

CRIME AND GUN CONTROL

Even President Reagan got into the act. "I can understand people being frustrated with the criminal justice system. But if they take the law into their own hands, that creates a breakdown in society."

What the President failed to understand was that he had it all backwards. First, society is already broken down, which, in effect, causes the actions of Bernhard Goetz.

In the tapes, Goetz described the system. "People commit crimes every day. They get away with them every day. New York City doesn't give a damn about violence. Otherwise this would have never happened. The city doesn't care about lawlessness, the government of New York City is a disgrace. The services are disgraceful. The subway system itself is a disaster. The school system is a disaster... I'm talking about the people, when they're deliberately maimed and they're beaten, and the powers that be, they fill in their paperwork and they shrug their shoulders and they turn their back and they have their cup of coffee. That is criminal negligence. The city doesn't care what happens to you. People who are violent are just let back out on the street again and again and they're charged with nothing."

The aspect of the trial which typified the upside down "Twilight Zone" nature of this debacle was the appearance of three of the "gentlemen" (as Prosecutor Waples called them) on the witness stand, testifying as the "victims."

Troy Canty, the one who first approached Goetz and demanded five dollars (he claims he "asked" for it), entered the courtroom all spiffy, in a well-tailored suit and tie. Commencing cross-examination, Goetz attorney Barry Slotnick presented a huge photo of the real Canty, a sneering hoodlum in street clothes, and cleverly placed it on an easel facing the jury.

Canty's testimony was a litany of repetition, "I don't remember", "I can't recall that", "Could you repeat that?" he repeated countless times. He had no credibility to begin with, and a savage in a suit and tie is still a savage. But to wipe out any doubt in the jurors' minds, Canty admitted under cross-examination that he had now given three different versions of the incident (the first to the grand jury, the second to Geraldo Rivera on ABC's "20/20"). He denied threatening the lives of a mother and her daughter. Both women were brought into court to help jar his failing memory.

He also denied making statements to two police officers who, later in the trial, confirmed that Canty admitted that the four intended to rob Goetz. To the first police officer on the scene of the crime, he said, "We were gonna rob the white guy but he shot us first." Two days later, in the hospital, Canty would only speak to a black transit cop. "We all stood around him because he looked 'soft,'" he conceded to Officer Charles Pennelton.

The second hoodlum in Goetz' line of fire, Barry Allen, was residing in prison at the time of the trial for chain-snatching, a crime he committed after the shooting.

SLOTNICK: "How are you today, Mr. Allen?"
ALLEN: "Fine."
SLOTNICK: "Where do you live?"
ALLEN: "Rikers Island."

The preceding exchange was the extent of Allen's testimony, as he proceeded to plead the fifth amendment 21 times to questions regarding the day of the shooting. This banter was conducted out of the presence of the jury, who were instructed that they may infer from Allen's absence that his testimony would have hurt the prosecution's case.

This was the first time that a *complainant* in an attempted murder trial felt that his testimony would be self-incriminating. Rod Serling would have loved it.

The first time James Ramseur entered the courtroom, he shocked the capacity crowd and shook up the jury with his menacing manner. Surrounded by court officers as he approached the witness stand, he shoved the Bible aside. "My client refuses to testify," his lawyer said. "It's not his choice," Judge Stephen Crane responded. "Mr. Ramseur, I order you to take the oath and testify."

"I refuse," Ramseur screamed as he glared at Crane. After being cited for contempt, he was led away. An obviously shaken jury thought they had seen the last of this terrifying figure. But the best was yet to come.

At the time, Ramseur was serving -- and continues to serve -- 8 1/3 to 25 years for the brutal rooftop rape of an 18 year-old pregnant black woman (a crime he committed two and a half months after the shooting and after Morgenthau granted him immunity from prosecution.) Feeling his multi-million dollar civil suit against Goetz (no joke) was further jeopardized by the contempt charge, he agreed to testify two weeks later. This set the stage for the most realistic representation for the jury of what precise element of society surrounded Bernhard Goetz on that fateful day.

Watching this hardened criminal place his hand on the Bible was a mockery and an insult, but it was certainly consistent with this circus of a trial. First, he admitted that in March of 1985 he faked his own kidnapping and sent the police on a wild goose chase. He claimed he was "set up" in his rape conviction by Slotnick and Goetz-supporter Roy Innis, the conservative black Chairman of the Congress of Racial Equality. The jurors were paid off, he said. The explosion was brewing.

Becoming more agitated with every question referring to previous crimes, Ramseur's hostility had jurors squirming in their seats. Screaming some of his answers but mumbling others, Judge Crane repeatedly asked Ramseur to speak into the microphone. "You want me to put it in my mouth?" he replied.

According to alternate juror Augustine Ayala, Ramseur's outburst was anticipated. "He had us terrified," he said. "We had a secret plan amongst ourselves to run out, to escape if he went crazy."

RAMSEUR: "I heard all about you."

SLOTNICK: "Nothing unpleasant I hope."

RAMSEUR: "It was all unpleasant."

SLOTNICK: "Prior to December 22, when was the last time you were with Darrell Cabey, Troy Canty, and Barry Allen?"

RAMSEUR: "When was the last time you got a drug dealer off?"

It then appeared Ramseur was removing his shoe to hurl it at Slotnick. Court officers surrounded him. Asked about the night before the shooting, which he spent with his girlfriend, Ramseur exploded. "It's none of your fuckin' business." Ordered to answer the question, he snapped, "It's none of your business either. He's playing fuckin' games. Take me outta here, Judge." Unfazed by the contempt warning, he replied, "With the time I'm doing, no time is gonna hurt me."

Ramseur had been called by the prosecution. By revealing his true self, he became the defense's star witness.

The most damaging evidence against Goetz was his own taped statement which described his so-called execution of Darrell Cabey. He stated that after firing all of the shots, he walked over to the wounded Cabey and said, "You seem to be doing alright. Here's another."

Every witness but one, however, claimed to have heard only a rapid-succession of shots taking no more than a second or two altogether. This greatly damaged the prosecution's contention that Goetz fired that solitary shot after the initial barrage.

A neuro-psychiatrist testified that Goetz may have been on "automatic pilot," a condition which develops from tremendous fear or anxiety. At the highest point of anxiety the body takes over and the mind is no longer in control. This testimony was used to demonstrate that Goetz emptied his gun immediately, had never fired that solitary shot, and, in fact, fantasized his shot at the seated Cabey. A ballistics expert testified that it would have been impossible for Cabey to have been seated when shot, since the bullet traveled parallel to the ground through his side and into the spine.

All of this is a necessary part of the antics in a courtroom. But in the arena of public morality and consensus, the issue is simply between hardened criminals and victims. And in that arena the consensus has always been overwhelmingly in favor of the true victim, Bernie Goetz.

What of the injuries suffered by Darrell Cabey? The bullet left him paralyzed and with brain damage. "Darrell Cabey cries out for justice!" Waples profoundly exclaimed in his summation. He also tried to elicit sympathy from the jury by having a surgeon describe the injuries in graphic detail.

While the civil jury bought into this nonsense in 1996, the criminal jury in 1987 did not. They understood that Darrell Cabey did not possess the moral authority to cry out for "justice." He had no right to cry out for anything. He was a hardened criminal who got what he deserved. He was robbing Bernhard Goetz. His injuries were a direct result of criminal activities, which sometimes contain risks. Those whose hearts bleed for Cabey have their sense of decency mixed up. They should be concerned with the *victims* of Darrell Cabey, those he's robbed, beaten, threatened, and terrified in his career as a violent street predator. Certainly, of all the pain inflicted on the streets and subways of New York, that suffered by Cabey was the least undeserved.

What the other witnesses revealed more than anything else was their intense fear of this gang of thugs. Andrea Reid, a black model, was seated on the train with her husband and infant child. As the gang began to hassle Goetz, she remarked to her husband, "Look at those punks picking on that white man." Later she told him, "They got what they deserved."

Mary Gant, an actress, her face recalling her tension, claimed she was "afraid and concerned." Again, when the police arrived and were about to track down the gunman, these were among the passengers who sent them in the *wrong* direction.

The only employee from Morgenthau's office who agreed to speak to me was Romy Gelles, an intern, who described herself as an "unapologetic liberal. I support tight gun control. The use of force was unnecessary," she said. "Besides, he could have just shown the gun."

This is a typical attack by those who apologize for criminals and fret at the thought of hoodlums having violent force turned on *them*. But her condemnation of Goetz did not stop with the gun issue.

"He would have been less likely to do that if they were white," she said. So there we have it. The familiar cry of racism from the DA's office.

Ironically, however, while the issue of race hovered over the case in terms of the wide publicity it received, it was never made an issue by Morgenthau's office as part of its prosecutorial strategy at the criminal trial. Prosecutor Waples dealt only with his convoluted interpretation of the case -- namely that Goetz acted recklessly and was a menace to society.

Of course, the only racism in the case -- besides four black hoodlums attacking a white man -- was that perpetrated by the New York system. "Compensatory racism" is one of the major factors which brought Bernhard Goetz to trial. This form of racism allows blacks to do what whites cannot do, in order to compensate for "prior injustices."

A man named Austin Weeks, branded the "black Bernie Goetz" by the Daily News, shot two white men whom he believed were robbing him. He killed one. As with Goetz, this occurred on the subway, an illegal gun was used, and he fled the scene. Weeks was rightly acquitted without even being indicted on the gun charge.

In 1986, a black token clerk, James Grimes, shot and killed a black mugger with an unlicensed weapon. Again, no indictments. What comes around, goes around, and Bernie Goetz was simply white at the wrong time.

In his summation, Waples referred to a previous robbery and beating suffered by Goetz as a "trivial encounter." The four criminals were "rambunctious kids." New York Post columnist Ray Kerrison described it accurately. "Gregory Waples insults our intelligence. Why in the name of decency should society surrender to predators like James Ramseur?"

"By a stroke of fortune, none of the youths died," Waples proclaimed. The girl raped and sodomized by Ramseur may have a second opinion.

The fundamental issue considered by the criminal trial jury was crime in New York City. The cross-section of New Yorkers -- eight whites, two blacks, two Hispanics -- understood the difference between good and evil, decency and indecency. The decision they made at the conclusion of the spectacular trial was a resounding victory for Goetz and law-abiding citizens everywhere. All the verdicts were "not guilty" except for the most minor possession charge.

Jubilation was everywhere, but four months later, in keeping with the political pressures of the day, the judge sentenced Goetz to a year in prison for a charge in which jail time is almost never given.

Muggers were delighted. Goetz served eight months and the case faded from the headlines for seven years.

Fast forward to 1996... Exactly one year ago this month, Darrell Cabey's civil trial against Goetz concluded with the $43 million award. In normal times, it would be preposterous for the "victims" in such a case even to dream of a monetary award for their heinous behavior. But, alas, these are not normal times. As Darrell Cabey's civil trial drew nearer, race became more and more of an issue -- not merely in terms of publicity but in legal strategy.

In the wake of the O.J. Simpson trial, it has become clear how juries work in a multi-racial society. In fact, as far back as the late 1970's, the now-deceased Bronx District Attorney Mario Merola, who prosecuted one of Goetz' assailants, admitted that it was becoming extremely difficult to get juries in the largely black county to convict blacks of violent crimes, and virtually impossible if the victims were white.

Cabey's attorney, Ronald Kuby, the radical disciple of the late William Kunstler, was not shy about what he intended to do in the courtroom. "The Manhattan jury in the criminal trial was white," he said. "Now we're in the Bronx and we know what we have to do."

Shortly before the trial, in a strange display of bad judgment, Goetz regretfully admitted in a national television talk show that when he was a young man he had gotten high on angel dust and made racial slurs. This admission forced his own lawyer to call Goetz a racist, but he implored the jury to award no damages since, in spite of this terrible quality, Goetz was still justified in the shooting.

There is no real dispute about why the all non-white jury awarded $43 million to a lifelong violent predator like Darrell Cabey. Goetz has been forced to transfer roughly 90 percent of his meager assets and will have to hand over a portion of his paycheck for the rest of his life. In a case that should have gone down in history as a triumph for the American spirit and system of justice, with the natural right of self-defense and common morality winning out, it instead will be recorded as yet another proof of why a multi-racial society cannot work.

Getting Away With Perjury

There is only one order of business not yet completed in the Bernhard Goetz affair. Why weren't hoodlums Troy Canty and James Ramseur indicted for perjury for their lying testimony at the Goetz criminal trial?

The initial reaction to this question must be: why weren't they indicted for attempted robbery? Surely, what happened on that subway car would be easy to prove. Forget it. These two "victims" were granted immunity from prosecution for all actions associated with that fateful day by Manhattan District Attorney Robert Morgenthau, the guardian and best friend of common criminals. No, even if they had openly admitted to extortion, Canty and Ramseur were securely protected by Morgenthau's office.

But perjury is a different matter. There are two basic classifications of perjury. The first is a sworn statement contradicted by one's own previous sworn statement. The second is a sworn statement contradicted by proven facts. Both types occurred as Canty and Ramseur disgraced the witness stand.

Indeed, it was amusing to me and embarrassing even to the most ardent enemies of Bernhard Goetz to watch Barry Allen, a complainant in an attempted murder charge, plead the fifth amendment twenty-one times. But do not be fooled. Allen was the wisest of the three choir boys to appear in court. He was the only one with the sense to keep his mouth shut.

Troy Canty's testimony, of course, was filled with hilarious contradictions. He was poorly coached, but coached nonetheless. Although he had given three different versions of the incident, he avoided a perjury charge by using a lawyer's trick. This legal cover, this technical escape became Canty's mantra throughout two entire days of testimony. When presented with his blatant contradictions, he would simply respond, "That's the way I remembered it then. I remember it differently now."

There exists, however, undeniable proof that Canty perjured himself through an outright lie by contradicting his own sworn statement the very next day. It was not something that immediately hit me, and I had to go through my notes in order to be certain, but I did request court transcripts that verified what I had already figured out.

During cross-examination by Goetz' attorney Barry Slotnick, Canty admitted that **for at least two years** he had a crack habit that cost him **$50 a day**. He further testified that **he did not work and supported this habit by robbing video machines.**

He had previously admitted that he had been **arrested for robbing video machines, shoplifting and selling stolen property**. However, the next day on the stand, Canty was asked if he had ever committed any crimes **besides the ones he was arrested for**. His reply? "No."

Freeze this testimony for a moment. A simple look at these straight-forward statements and simple math prove perjury beyond the shadow of a doubt.

On one hand, Canty admits that his drug habit ran him thousands of dollars ($50 a day for at least two years) which he admits he supported only through robbery because he did not work. Conversely, he swears the only crimes he ever committed were those on official record (which he was arrested for) which had a net financial profit of zero. These statements do not square!

No action was ever taken by the DA when this was brought to his attention.

In addition to Canty proving his own lie, both he and Ramseur perjured themselves based on their testimony that *Canty and only Canty* approached Bernhard Goetz on that subway car while the others stayed a reasonable distance away.

Several witnesses testified that at least three men approached Goetz. Still, it is one thing for the common observer to consider this proof of perjury. But, lo and behold, Morgenthau's prosecutor, Gregory Waples, clearly stated in his summation that he believed these witnesses.

Why?

Goetz had described to police on both audio and videotape his so-called, now-famous execution of Darrell Cabey (when after shooting all of the perpetrators, he approached Cabey and said, "You seem to be doing alright. Here's another.") It was proven in court that this never actually happened.

In a desperate but ironic maneuver, Waples needed to convince the jury to *believe Goetz' version* of the incident in order to convict him on the so-called execution of Cabey. In order to do this, he outsmarted himself by telling the jury how credible these witnesses were, since they corroborated Goetz' version.

Waples stated, "The defendant said that Troy Canty and Barry Allen both came over to him. Troy Canty said that as far as he knows, he alone approached the defendant, but you know the defendant's version is accurate because at least three independent witnesses have said that they saw two persons standing over the defendant before the shots were fired. Josephine Holt saw that; Garth Reid saw that; Mary Gant saw that."

In other words, the District Attorney's office has publicly stated that it believes Goetz' description of the incident and concurs that at least three of the punks approached Bernie Goetz. In still other words, Morgenthau's office officially believes, through Waples' summation, that Canty and Ramseur were lying when they said that only Canty approached.

If proof beyond a reasonable doubt is needed to convict, only probable cause is needed to indict. And in these cases of perjury, a second grand jury, which Morgenthau is so fond of convening, would not have been necessary.

Freedom and the Brady Law

The Brady Law — the farce legislation which mandates a 15-day waiting period before the purchase of a handgun — has just turned four years old. The confiscators of freedom — otherwise known as gun control advocates — are whooping it up, celebrating the birthday of this monstrous sham in much the same manner they would fawn over Rosemary's Baby.

Touting the nation's drop in crime as proof that the law is working, gun controllers have consistently paraded false numbers and results to bolster their propaganda machine. Ever since James Brady was disabled by John Hinckley's bullet during the Reagan assassination attempt, Brady and especially his wife Sarah have dedicated their lives to destroying the freedom of others. Much like newcomer Carolyn McCarthy, whose husband was murdered by Colin Ferguson in the Long Island Railroad massacre, the Bradys have used their personal tragedy to garner sympathy for an evil cause.

Gun control has never been much more than the pet panacea of deluded liberals who are determined to shed the image that they are soft on crime. Advocating for gun control is the pathetic attempt to pretend they are making a tangible contribution to the war on crime. Violent street criminals are infinitely grateful for the help gun controllers have given them whilst plying their nefarious trade. Indeed, an unarmed populace creates a much more conducive climate for the business of rapists and muggers. Criminals are, therefore, the most ardent supporters and giddy beneficiaries of tight gun control, of which waiting periods are an important part.

What are the real numbers regarding the Brady Law? Bill Clinton, who has perfected the art of the "lawyer's" answer to straight-forward questions, claims, as does Janet Reno, that 100,000 applicants have been prevented from purchasing pistols due to the "success" of the police background checks conducted during the waiting period. As usual, there is a grain of truth to the President's misleading words, which come unraveled upon closer inspection. Certainly, 100,000 applicants have been denied their constitutional rights because of Brady. The only problem is that it has been proven that some 90,000 (!) of these rejections were caused by mistaken identity, traffic offenses and other computer errors.

In reality, therefore, only 10,000 rejections have been "legitimate." And of these 10,000 the vast majority of denials resulted from non-violent crimes committed by the applicants many years ago. The notion that hardened criminals, who break every law from petty larceny to murder, will actually go to the trouble of purchasing a weapon legally and submit to a background check is something that only the mind of a gun controller can be totally at ease with. Only fools believe that the Brady Law — or any gun control law — prevents criminals from obtaining weapons.

Waiting periods not only fail at their purported mission, they actually increase crime and cost innocent lives. The quintessential example was the Los Angeles riots in 1992. (Before the federal Brady Law, California had its own state version.) During these horrible days of lawless mayhem, looting, rampaging and murder, terrified citizens seeking to protect their lives and their property flocked to gun stores and were told they had to *wait*. Left naked to assault and denied their right to bear arms because of the waiting period, an inhuman savagery was inflicted upon law-abiding citizens by predators who did not have to wait.

Moreover, the failure of waiting periods, rather than wake gun control tyrants from their delusions, has always been used as an excuse for *yet longer waiting periods*. California went from 2 days in 1940; to 3 days in 1958; to 5 days in 1965; to 15 days in 1976. During that period, violent crime rose steadily, peaking at a 400 percent increase. During the glory days of the Dinkins mayoralty and the Crown Heights riots in New York, the waiting period for a first-time handgun purchase was four to six *months*. Big help.

In a landmark victory for freedom and the Tenth Amendment, the Supreme Court last year struck down the provision of the Brady Law that required the states to conduct background checks, on the grounds that the federal government cannot tell states how to spend their money. To no surprise, crime has not increased in the locales where the background check has been eliminated. Undeterred, gun controllers have fought to enact state versions of the bill which cost taxpayers millions of wasted dollars on useless paperwork, and police man-hours devoted to checking on honest citizens rather than patrolling the streets.

Despite the hoopla, gun controllers have never been able to correlate the effects of the Brady Law with the drop in crime, which is in reality due to demographic shift — the aging of the population.

The real effects of the Brady Law and all gun control legislation are to increase crime and to trample on the precious freedom articulated in the Second Amendment. The real agenda is the *ultimate confiscation* of all privately-owned weapons and the loss of freedom. Pray for Rosemary's Baby.

The Color of Crime

The preponderance of violent crime in the United States over the past three decades has profoundly altered the entire fabric of American life. In any local or national survey, the specter of rampant violence invariably appears at the top of peoples' concerns. Liberal Supreme Court rulings and the fatally misguided belief in "rehabilitation" of criminals led to weak law enforcement policies which contributed immeasurably to the growth in violent crime.

Crime, therefore, is accurately categorized as a social issue. But it is also a *political* issue, which means that when crime is deliberated upon publicly, its unspoken and most glaring factor is ignored. The factor, of course, is race.

The crime problem, on the surface, appears to be simply a matter of laws, courts and cultural standards. But a close examination just *beneath the surface* reveals the racial component of crime to be definitive. A city's racial composition will determine more about its crime situation than local law enforcement policies. No responsible examination of crime can be done without looking at it through the prism of race. Still, the third rail of American politics deliberately goes unmentioned.

How much violent crime is there in America and who is committing it? How common is interracial crime and which race is more victimized by it? The answers to these questions can readily be obtained in yearly volumes released by the Department of Justice. For the faint of heart and the politically correct, the findings are very disturbing. It is no secret why the government and "mainstream" journalists make no effort to publicize the inconvenient results.

People without blinders on already know, through their own observations, that blacks proportionately commit most of the violent crime in America. The actual numbers are staggering. Although blacks are only 13 percent of the population, they commit nearly 60 percent of the murders. Blacks, therefore, are 8.5 times more likely than whites to commit murder. So blacks, *all by themselves*, account for the fact that the United States has a higher murder rate than England or Italy. And this is the *narrowest* rate of racial difference by crime. The rates for rapes, robberies and gang assaults are even wider. Blacks are 11 times more likely than whites to commit rape; 17 times more likely to commit robbery or "mugging"; and 22 times more likely to commit a gang assault or robbery.

Interracial crime is the source of certain misconceptions. Judging by the hysterical publicity given the instances — real or imagined — of white-on-black crime, one would believe these occurrences to be widespread. They are, in fact, very rare. Racial orthodoxy dictates that the maximum public scrutiny be granted whenever whites victimize blacks. Front-page news is always followed by national breast-beating, soul searching, self-analysis and discussions of "white racism."

On the other hand, when blacks victimize whites, the media go to pains to avoid mentioning the race of the victim or perpetrator. If the races become known, the motivation for the crime is never described as racial.

The actual lopsided disparities in interracial crime rates are nothing less than breathtaking. Black-on-white murder is 17 times more likely than white-on-black murder; black-on-white robbery and rape are both 70 times more likely than the reverse; and black-on-white gang violence is 83 times more likely. (These numbers are actually even worse than they appear because Hispanics are included in the "white" perpetrator totals, thereby exaggerating the white crime rates.)

On the rare occasions that the horrible rate of black crime is publicly discussed, the myth of black-on-black crime comes into play. This falsehood, which is unfortunately also spouted by many uninformed conservatives, basically states that while there is definitely an inordinate amount of black crime, it is blacks themselves who are overwhelmingly the victims of it. Not so. Excepting murder, whites are chosen by blacks as victims more than half the time, so *there is actually more black-on-white crime than black-on-black crime.*

One-third of all black men between the ages of 15 and 30 are caught up in the criminal justice system in one form or another (in prison, on parole, on probation or on the lam.) While apologists for the black criminal element try to explain this all away by suggesting the police and the courts are racist, honest observers know that the black crime rate is so high for the simple reason that blacks are committing most of the crimes. We hear often that the death penalty is applied in a discriminatory manner. It sure is. The white rate of execution is actually slightly higher than the black rate.

It is amusing to watch public and high profile people deny or avoid their own senses, especially when the facts are irrefutable by any objective standard. Race is clearly the single best indicator of a location's probable crime numbers. Liberals may deplore this, but the lack of honest discussion will only allow the violence to continue, while the obvious truth continues to be muzzled.

Race and the Death Penalty

One of the most enduring myths in contemporary discussions of the death penalty is the notion that executions in the United States are implemented in a racially discriminatory manner. What is remarkable about the durability of this falsehood is the fact that there is not now — nor has there ever been — even the flimsiest of evidence to substantiate it.

Racial paranoids who propagate the charge that blacks are executed at a higher rate than whites make their "case" by spouting the standard accusations about the criminal justice system being hopelessly racist. The same charges of bias supposedly explain why so many blacks are arrested and are in prison — never mind that blacks are simply committing most of the crimes. (One prominent black refuses to use the word "justice" and instead has coined the term "criminal *processing* system." The expression is said to be catching on amongst blacks.)

Consideration of race in executions came closest to becoming public policy in 1994 when Bill Clinton, kowtowing to the Congressional Black Caucus, promised that federal prosecutors would apply a racial standard to their efforts — namely that unless the racial composition of condemned prisoners reflected that of the general population, they would not pursue the death penalty. This promise came on the heels of the defeat of the Racial Justice Act which would have legally required quotas in executions. Consideration of evidence, jury deliberations and the circumstances of heinous crimes would all take a back seat to affirmative action.

It does not require a calculus degree to sift through the numbers. Since blacks commit murders at a rate eight times that of whites, and Asian-Americans rarely commit any, there can never be the kind of perfect symmetry the Racial Justice Act would have required. Capital punishment, therefore, would have effectively been eliminated. The National District Attorneys Association called the Act "a vote to end the death penalty."

The numbers put out by the Bureau of Justice Statistics demolish all the hysterical claims of race bias against blacks in sentencing. In the most recent survey, 6.9 percent of convicted whites received life sentences, compared to 7.1 percent for blacks and 6.7 percent for Hispanics. The percentage of inmates serving life without parole was identical for whites and blacks (0.7 percent). Most significantly, the percentage of convicted whites receiving the death penalty was 0.5; for blacks it was 0.3; and for Hispanics 0.4 percent. Thus far, the rates appear identical. A closer examination, however, reveals race bias *in favor of blacks.*

While 59 percent of death row inmates were white, 39 percent were black, even though blacks commit more than half the nation's murders. Therefore, blacks are *considerably underrepresented* on death row. The numbers are relatively the same for actual executions. Since 1977, only 43 percent of those executed have been black. So if a racial quota was actually applied based on the number of convicted murderers, rather than on percentages of the population, those clamoring for the Racial Justice Act would find themselves in the awkward position of advocating more executions of blacks.

In the rare instances when this bad news actually penetrates the racial bean counters, they resort to an interesting argument with a different racial twist. Although black murderers are no more likely to be executed than white murderers, they say, blacks will still receive the death penalty at a higher rate when they kill whites than when they kill other blacks — concluding that this is because society simply places a higher value on a white life.

This phenomenon, however, is caused not by institutional racism, but by the fact that when blacks murder whites, it is overwhelmingly during the kinds of crimes to which the death penalty applies. Murders which involve people of different races are almost always committed by strangers. These types of murders usually involve burglary or robbery, qualifying for the death penalty because of the double felony charges. Black on black murder (the most common type of murder) is normally drug, gang or family-related — cases that do not typically result in the death penalty. But when blacks kill whites, it is frequently in the context of burglary or robbery. White on white murder is statistically split between double felony and family-related types. White on black murder is almost non-existent, despite the attendant media publicity when one occurs.

It is a damning commentary on current public discourse that opponents of capital punishment, lacking a genuine coherent case against the death penalty, can resort to such a transparent argument as race bias and still receive a serious hearing from policymakers. When race enters the equation, logic becomes secondary to hysteria.

Gun Locks: The New Chic Craze

First it was waiting periods. Then it was background checks. Next came the "assault rifle" ban. Let's not forget registration. Then bullet identification numbers. Confiscation, of course. Then the crackdown on "Saturday Night Specials." Ban on semi-automatics...

It's hard to be chic trying to keep up with the latest fads on the gun controllers' stylish agenda. When one craze becomes passe', the confiscators can always be counted on to come up with another. So just as the mood ring replaced the hoola hoop, the new hip cause that will save America's children from those evil gun owners is the gun lock.

Just as when the Hustle came out, anyone who's anyone is in on it. There is currently proposed federal legislation, as well as state and local bills in different stages of metastasizing that will harass law-abiding handgun owners, while the criminals are hysterical laughing. But the liberals, on a certain level, ought to be admired for their relentless consistency in the face of total failure. If liberalism is the religion, gun control is the First Gospel. In *The Honeymooners*, when Alice Kramden was criticizing one of Ralph's notorious slip-ups in his hair-brained get-rich-quick schemes, he retorted, "No one's one hundred percent, Alice." She replied, "You are. You've been wrong every time."

And so it is with the new pursuit of mandatory gun locks. The proposed laws require that all handguns be attached with trigger locks, which will supposedly keep children from killing themselves or others in horrible accidents. These types of accidents are almost non-existent, but gun control shills in liberal political circles play them up to give the false impression that they happen on a routine basis. It is important to understand that gun controllers are among the most shameless statistical liars. Their numbers can simply never be believed. For example, bicycles kill far more children than handguns, but Americans will look long and hard to see the actual numbers on the fingertips of the confiscators.

Furthermore, when gun control advocates trot out the statistics claiming a high number of "children" being killed by firearms, the definition of "children" is the one created by federal authorities, which is under the age of 18. So when two 17 year old hoodlum drug addicts in the ghetto *intentionally* shoot each other between fixes, this counts as "children" being killed by handguns, with the image of a toddler reaching into his father's gun rack.

Having failed to effectively disarm all law-abiding Americans, gun controllers seek to render the guns they own useless. Most of the mental midgets voting for these laws wouldn't know a gun lock from a wrist watch, but they understand how to trample on the rights of honest people and get tough — not on criminals — but on inanimate objects. The whole point of having a defensive weapon in one's home is for quick, life-saving access and use in the event of criminal intrusion. Gun locks cause critical time to be lost. Ever try opening the house mail box in the middle of the night?

The recent well-publicized study by Professor John Lott of the University of Chicago, "More Guns, Less Crime," proved what all sensible people already knew: the presence of guns in honest hands deters criminals and saves innocent lives. In all locales nationwide where right-to-carry laws were enacted since the mid-1980's, crime went *down*. Americans defend themselves more than 760,000 times annually against violent predators with legally owned firearms.

But the gun lock craze has an even more sinister side. The legal theory of Strict Liability defines guilt as simply having committed the illegal act, regardless of mitigating circumstances. For example, a man is guilty of statutory rape by having sex with a minor, even if he had every reason to believe she was 30. Similarly, running a red light is always an offense, even if one is rushing a child to the emergency room. As a corollary to this gun control madness, gun controllers want to require that citizens act "responsibly" (get gun locks), but at the same time want to apply Strict Liability to such laws, so that even if owners purchase and attach the locks, they will still be held responsible in the event of an accident. Perhaps more importantly, they are pushing this theory independent of whether gun lock legislation passes. This is intended to terrify people out of owning guns. So far, courts have rejected this nonsense. But totalitarians never stop trying.

They also never stop believing in the Instrumentality Theory, which holds that the mere presence itself of instruments (guns) causes violence. Gun ownership has risen 50 percent in the past decade. As Prof. Lott's study shows, however, not only has violent crime gone down in that period, it has decreased most substantially where gun ownership has risen most sharply. But religious fanatics rely on faith, not facts. So gun controllers will continue their passionate crusade for the gun lock. The hoola hoop should be returning any day now.

6
EDUCATION

The Bilingual Follies

Of all the disastrous forms of multi-lingualism in America today, the most notorious is bilingual education. The calamity which began in the late 1960's as a $7.5 million federal program to teach Mexican children to speak English, has metastasized into a colossal behemoth costing American taxpayers $5.5 billion annually. New York City alone spends over $400 million a year on its roughly 150,000 bilingual-taught students. The dollars would be better spent lining bird cages. Bilingualism is not only a financial disaster. It is also an educational and cultural one.

What started (theoretically) as a means to promote English among foreign pupils, has in reality become nothing more than a form of cultural rebellion for radical America-hating activists, who are actually using it to promote Spanish among Hispanic children, *even if they only speak English.* One of the most common stories is that of Miguel Alvarado, whose 8-year old daughter was placed in a bilingual class simply because of her Hispanic surname. "We don't even speak Spanish at home," he said. This radical agenda is revealed more explicitly in the Los Angeles Unified School District's *Bilingual Methodology Study Guide*, which instructs teachers "not to encourage minority parents to switch to English in the home, but to encourage them to strongly promote development of the primary language."

The theory of bilingualism — which was to teach students in both their so-called native language and English — has been thrown out the window. Bilingualism has become in reality monolingualism — only the native language is taught. According to radical Josue Gonzalez, director of bilingual education during the Carter administration, Spanish "should no longer be regarded as a 'foreign' language.'" It should be, he says, "a second national language." At the annual conference of the National Association for Bilingual Education, many speakers actually challenged the idea of United States sovereignty by endorsing the formation of a separate nation in the American Southwest called *La Frontera*. Mexican flags often adorn such gatherings. All this should provide an accurate reflection of the mentality of rabid bilingualists.

In New York City, the bilingual follies know no bounds. In the last ten years, public school children have been taught in over 80 different languages! Some of the more well-known tongues include Kpelle, Nyanja, Twi, Gurma, Cham, Ga, Khowan, Bemba, Ibo, Oriya, and Ewe.

Huh?

Ewe, in fact, is a very interesting case. It is spoken in parts of Togo, a small country in West Africa. The Togolese themselves do not even offer public school instruction in Ewe. That is because *it cannot be written down.* This has created a bit of a problem for New York City's bilingual education bureaucrats, who are wondering why they cannot find any Ewe textbooks. The politically incorrect Togolese teach French, the language of the colonizer. All of this merely shows that any foreigner, speaking any obscure language, can arrive in New York and demand instruction in his native language. It also means that teachers must be imported, once the bilingual establishment figures out where Kpelle, Nyanja and Ibo are actually spoken.

The only fools who claim to still believe in bilingual education, in addition to cultural radicals, are the financial beneficiaries of the bilingual bureaucracy. Bilingual education has always operated under a sort of "reverse Darwinism," in Thomas Sowell's words — the survival of the unfittest. The more it fails, the more it is claimed to be needed. Every scientifically valid study has shown that immersion in English — allowing students to sink or swim in all-English classes — is the only method of effective assimilation.

Rosalie Pedalino Porter, the former director of bilingual education in Newton, Massachusetts, writes in her critique, *Forked Tongue: The Politics of Bilingual Education,* "I felt that I was deliberately holding back the learning of English." Gail Fiber, an elementary school teacher with seven years experience in bilingual ed, said, "...I've never seen it done successfully. How can anyone learn English in school when they speak Spanish four hours a day.?" Columnist Linda Chavez reports that even tenured teachers have told her that "they do not speak out against bilingual education for fear of being labeled as racists."

The salaries of bilingualists in the public schools are being used to undermine the United States and prevent children from learning English. The documentation of its failure is so thorough that opposition to bilingualism now cuts across most ideological lines. At one time, the immigrant was expected to conform. Now, the burden continues to fall on the American taxpayers, who are forced to subsidize the supplanting of their own language and their own country.

School Desegregation: Judicial Tyranny

It is considered nothing less than heresy to criticize the most hallowed decision ever rendered by the Supreme Court, the order to desegregate the public schools issued in *Brown v. Topeka Board of Education* in 1954. Even many who are old enough to have opposed it at the time, now say they support it. This has happened in spite of the fact that the movement to integrate the public schools became a tyrannical crusade resulting in abject disaster, failing at every one of its original promises.

The *Brown* decision as pure legal reasoning was a monstrous mockery of Constitutional law, and dictatorial judicial activism at its most mischievous. In theory (but no longer in practice) the Supreme Court's job is merely to interpret the Constitution and the law — not to legislate based on its own fanciful desires for society. The Court has, at different times, interpreted the Constitution to permit segregated schools, forbid them completely, then allow them in certain circumstances.

The truth — and it is as certain a legal verity as any honest reading permits — is that the Constitution is totally silent on the subject of segregation, and judges have simply read their own ideological views into it.

The impetus for the 1954 ruling was largely based on a social science doctrine called the "harm and benefit thesis" which gave rise to the notion that if schools were "separate" they were "unequal." Segregation, the theory went, was caused by white prejudice and resulted in black feelings of inferiority. This caused degrading circumstances and low standards for blacks. Whites then pointed to the black situation to justify their own prejudices, and on and on this cycle continued. To break the cycle, integration would be the cure, blacks would improve their lot, and whites would set aside their prejudices which, according to the theory, were the only obstacle to equal achievement for blacks.

The 1954 Court was also profoundly influenced by the studies of black psychologist Kenneth Clark who found that black children attending segregated schools, when given a choice between a black doll and a white doll, more often chose the white doll. This was offered as "proof" that segregation caused black self-esteem problems. It is now known that Clark refrained from telling the Court that blacks attending integrated schools chose the white doll at an even higher rate than at segregated schools, which, assuming the doll test had any worth, would demonstrate that segregation was *good* for blacks.

With the Court about to usher in a brave new world based on the reasoning presented before it, the assumption was that desegregation and then integration would send blacks on the road to full equality. But the ruling itself only outlawed *de jure* segregation, it did not specifically *require* integration. With housing patterns remaining segregated because of peoples' choices, schools by and large remained segregated. That all changed with *Green v. New Kent County* in 1968 and, more ominously, *Swann v. Charlotte-Mecklenburg* in 1971 which introduced forced school busing.

While the results of all this social tinkering were supposed to be racial harmony and black equality in achievement, reality, over the course of the last 40 years, has told a much more cruel and stark story. What forced integration did, more than anything else, was bring about a "white flight" to the suburbs of historic proportions.

Similarly, whites moved their children to private schools in record numbers. Today, public schools are so overwhelmingly non-white, that blacks have scarcely more white schoolmates than they did in 1968, when the integration madness gained full steam.

Rather than improve black test scores, the gap between the races has remained stubbornly constant. The nonsensical claim that black schools have been slighted in the allocation of resources has also been disproven, removing yet another excuse for dismal performance. The "harm and benefit thesis" has been exposed as sociological claptrap, with blacks generally showing *higher* self-esteem than whites in studies. Integration, contrary to the original theory, lowers self-esteem for blacks.

With the "harm and benefit thesis" no longer mentioned, the Supreme Court backtracked somewhat in 1991, stating that as long as segregation was merely the result of natural housing patterns and school districts did not deliberately keep the races apart, schools need not forcibly be racially adjusted by court order. Still, many schools have acquiesced to the shrill hysterics of those who claim the 40 year effort had not gone *far enough*. Some have done away with grouping students by ability, imposed radical racial and ethnic studies and sometimes even eliminated grades altogether in the interests of "harmony."

The integrationist experiment has failed by colossal proportions in every one of its purported objectives. Even the NAACP has now conceded that integration is not necessarily a desirable end. But it was always those politicians and jurists who least had to live with the effects of forced integration who have always been its chief proponents.

Abolish Public Education

Leonid Brezhnev once said that socialism was irreversible and to a large extent he was right. Once leaches get their mitts on the public dole — other people's money obtained through coercion — the inertia to stay addicted to taxpayer largess defies all other laws of science and nature. It would be easier to reverse a tidal wave.

With massive social bureaucracies in place, only legislators can cut down the size of government through the power of law — something they invariably are too spineless to do. Even the Republican Congress, which was elected on the promise to not only slash programs but to take the bolder and more radical step of *eliminating* agencies altogether, has basically sold out. The pornographic National Endowment for the Arts has just gotten approval for another $98 million to fund, among other things, a play depicting Jesus as a homosexual.

But the most scandalous social jobs program, the one that has done the most damage and stands as a national monument to incompetence and waste is America's public education system. It is time to abolish it. There are two basic cases for the abolition of public education. One is the theoretical-constitutional case in principle. The other is pragmatic. Each could stand on its own. Taken together, the case is devastating. (Gun control laws serve as an effective example. They are plainly unconstitutional, but the fact that they also fail in practice makes it easier to argue the case politically.)

The libertarian case against public education is simply that government is best which governs least. Government has no place in education anymore than it has a place in changing light bulbs, cleaning carpets or making pizza. No one can really justify or offer a rationale as to why government is even involved in education, other than to state "it always has been." This is similar to the matter of first class mail, where the federal government has always had a monopoly on delivery, but no one knows why. People are simply used to it and accept it.

While government involvement in education on the state and local level is not unconstitutional, it is still a violation of libertarian and Jeffersonian principle. Federal involvement, however, is a gross and blatant violation of the Constitution. Congressman Ron Paul introduced a bill in the House which would have eliminated all federal funding not specifically permitted by the Constitution. It received 54 votes.

The practical case against public education is revealed in its disastrous record. Explaining why America needs to eliminate the public education system is like explaining why it needs to eliminate cholera or locusts. The system is bankrupt — educationally, intellectually and morally. In fact, it is bankrupt in every way except financially, as it is the squandering recipient of billions of taxpayer dollars which would be used more effectively lining bird cages. Illiteracy is at an all-time high. The system has failed in its most elementary duty — teaching children to read and write. Yet pointy-headed educrats have taken it upon themselves to delve into the area of amateur psychology, pushing ridiculous "self-esteem" programs, pornographic sex education and anti-American multiculturalism.

Private schools always outperform public schools while spending far less. This is largely due to the fact that incompetents are attracted to the public education system. Public school educators are America's worst.

Recent examples of this in the news tell very familiar stories. In Massachusetts, a test of applicants for teaching positions revealed an extraordinarily low level of knowledge — 60 percent failed — and questons like "Define a preposition" had them scratching their heads. Commenting on what he terms "the high price of allowing [these] shallow people to set the norms in our public schools," Thomas Sowell remarked, "Dumbness is dangerous. And tenured dumbness is doubly dangerous." Columnist Gary Wills writes, "...one thing [about public schools] we were not until now supposed to mention is that they have bad teachers."

A school district in Suffolk County gave teaching applicants an 11th grade reading test which three-quarters of them failed. One-third of applicants failed a basic-skills test in Virginia. Such horror stories permeate the public education system, including the fact that half the math and science teachers in California were discovered to have no training in those subjects. Clearly, it would be an understatement to assert that incompetency is rampant and stupidity abounds in the public education system. Indeed, while the system routinely graduates illiterates who cannot read their own diplomas, it also employs teachers who can only charitably be characterized as dullards.

And teachers are notorious whiners — constantly demanding more money and benefits for jobs poorly done. Despite the myth that teachers are underpaid, a study by the Educational Intelligence Agency reports that since teachers work only an average of 185 days a year, compared to 235 for everyone else, they do, when factoring in this inconvenient data, earn more than the average worker in all 50 states! The pay discrepancy is so drastic that teachers' pay exceeds all other workers by *more than 25 percent* in every state but two.

Naturally, the teachers' unions, which oppose tax vouchers and are terrified of any sort of competition for their corrupt system, also oppose testing of teachers. Most parents who send their children to public schools do so for the same reason people ride New York City's subways — because they have no other choice. No one *wants* to send their children to public schools.

It is no surprise, given their miserable records, that public school educators are also very cowardly. Those who have risked their careers to do the right thing are scarcer than hen's teeth. Even politicians, of all people, have demonstrated greater courage than this sorry lot. Regrettably, even the best people in public education would not support its elimination since one would need to be approaching sainthood to advocate the abolition of one's living. Push illiteracy and pick up that paycheck.

There is no case — neither constitutional nor pragmatic — for the continued existence of public education. The only justification left is that it is easier for totalitarians to control a "dumbed-down" populace and, perhaps, to provide employment for the simple-minded.

The Sex Education Racket: A Politically Correct Guide

Introduction

Once again, the radical homosexual lobby has achieved one of its political victories by escaping blame for its most horrible legacy, AIDS. The anti-academic educational establishment is also celebrating the publication of yet another monument to the promotion of illegitimacy, sexually transmitted diseases, and rampant sexual activity by twelve year-olds. The gods of Political Correctness are not only producing more material far too explicit for students, but are engaging in more brainwashing and left-wing indoctrination. And condom-mania is running wild, complete with the so-called "success rates" and demonstrations, too.

All of this has been accomplished with the New York City Board of Education's **HIV/AIDS Curriculum Guide, Grades 7-9**. The subtitle of this monstrous slap at traditional moral values is "A Supplement to a Comprehensive Health Curriculum." It would be more properly titled "The Politically Correct Homosexual Protection Guide." While giving lip service to "abstinence," the guide is a blatant promotion of promiscuity. Regarding the guide, Thomas Sobol, the former left-wing State Commissioner of Education, has written that it provides "accurate" materials and information. Accurate? Writing about the causes and transmission of AIDS without blaming perverse homosexual behavior is akin to writing on the Holocaust without blaming Nazism.

Why Sex Education at all?

It is unfortunate, but all too frequently when the conventional wisdom is dead wrong, there are still many otherwise sensible people who buy into it. Such is the case with the "sex education" phenomenon that has infested the school systems since the 1970's.

This conventional wisdom, usually without any challenge, states that sex education is a necessity given the modern climate. It goes further, with nary a rebuttal, that providing sex education to students will, ipso facto, reduce the pregnancy rate among teenagers and help stem the tide against sexually transmitted diseases (STDs). Children must be told about the availability of condoms, shown how to use them, and be further instructed in "safe sex" techniques, the conventional wisdom holds. In layman's terms, the conventional wisdom states, "Well, we must deal with reality and reality tells us that kids are going to do it anyway, so we might as well make it as safe as possible and inform them as much as possible." This conventional wisdom is practically monolithic in the education establishment. The truth, of course, tells an entirely different story. Sex education is not a solution, but is part of the problem.

The great educator and writer Thomas Sowell has written that sex education is among "psycho-therapeutic activities [which have] flourished in the public schools — without any evidence of their effectiveness for their avowed purposes, and *even despite accumulating evidence of their counterproductive effects...*" (emphasis added.)

A mere look at the facts supports Sowell's assertion and demolishes the conventional wisdom. There is an old saying: When you want less of something, you tax it; when you want more of something, you subsidize it. Clearly, by providing "education" in sexual matters beyond mere parental instruction and guidance, there is condoning and encouragement going on, whether intended or not. Allowing instructions in condoms, techniques and "safety," has always served to increase the sexual activity among teenagers substantially. Before the 1970's, the "heyday of the growth of sex education," teenage pregnancy was declining over a period which extended beyond the previous decade. The pregnancy rate was roughly 68 per thousand. Venereal diseases were comparatively low. All of this was before "sex education" exploded onto the scene of public education thanks to massive federal funding.

At that point, parents were told that sex education would reduce the rates of teenage pregnancy and venereal diseases. (Now, they are told it will reduce the transmission of AIDS.) Upon sex education's rapid spread in the public schools in the 1970's, out-of-wedlock teenage pregnancies *rose* — and rose sharply. While there was no evidence that a majority of teenagers were engaging in sex before the rise of sex education, there is ample evidence that they do now. And all this activity came on the heels of the "sex education" explosion.

In addition, "sex education" implies a biological or scientific bent which in reality it does not have, at least not in its most common form. What it does have is a liberal sociological bent — brainwashing and indoctrination — which will be documented in the subsequent pages regarding this HIV/AIDS Curriculum Guide. The guide is more concerned with the re-shaping of the children's attitudes with politically correct nonsense than with scientific truths. Usually, the indoctrination is totally contrary to what the parents would have their children believe.

Finally, and perhaps most importantly, sex education has usurped the power and authority of the individual parents to decide *when and if* such instructions are necessary for their own children, taking into account the individual child's unique emotional development. All of the empirical evidence shows that parental influence and their moral values are a more effective force against the spread of sexually transmitted diseases than the nutty liberal psycho-babble cooked up by the amateur "psychologists" comprising the education establishment.

The Homosexual Coverup

The radical homosexual lobby has scored a major victory with the publishing of this guide for several reasons. First of all, why in the world should there be an AIDS curriculum at all? For the same reason that Hollywood leftists and other assorted politically correct oddballs wear red ribbons. AIDS has become the chic cause of the '90s. Other diseases cause infinitely more deaths, yet only AIDS gets the massive funding, celebrity endorsements and special attention in school curriculum. Obviously, the reason actions such as fighting against AIDS, lobbying for more money, and having curriculum placed in the schools is fashionable is because the disease overwhelmingly affects homosexuals. It's their cause for evident reasons of self-interest.

But homosexuals have performed a rather remarkable feat with all this AIDS business. They have managed to focus all this attention and political muscle on AIDS, without taking the blame for its existence and horrible spread. Homosexual culpability in the transmission of AIDS is so outrageously total that to discuss AIDS and its transmission without pointing the finger almost exclusively at homosexual behavior is the new Big Lie. As mentioned earlier, it is tantamount to discussing the Holocaust without blaming Nazism. Yet ignore the homosexual role is exactly what the guide does.

When AIDS first reared its ugly head in the early 1980's, it soon became known as the "gay disease." The homosexual lobby labored tirelessly to try and portray AIDS as "everyone's disease." In spite of the falseness of that premise, the radical lobby was quite successful, to the point where many people today fear that AIDS is a plague which affects everyone. The reason the radicals knew they had to pretend AIDS was a disease like any other, able to strike any segment of the general population, was for funding purposes. They understood full well that the American public would never support massive amounts of tax dollars being poured into the coffers of a disease which was almost exclusively the province of homosexuals and intravenous drug users. More significantly, they knew Americans would be further reluctant when knowing that it was the grossly irresponsible and perverse behavior of those groups that was spreading the disease. The radical homosexuals wanted to focus on the relatively few examples of those infected with the disease through blood transfusions (truly innocent people including children.) Most of the media cooperated in this charade. Only when accomplishing this end could funding be attained at the astronomical level it has.

The numbers are indisputable. Contrary to the propaganda, AIDS is not "breaking out" into the general population. It has, in fact, leveled off. The wild predictions of millions dead never came to fruition. The disease has not spread to the heterosexual population. It is, in fact, the "gay disease" everyone thought it was. It is not nearly the mass killer that cancer and heart disease are. Since the beginning of the epidemic, AIDS has taken roughly 90,000 lives. But 40,000 women die of breast cancer *every year*. More than a million Americans are diagnosed with cancer yearly, with half dying from it. Three quarters of a million people will die of heart disease yearly. Yet AIDS receives more than $2 billion annual funding — more than both cancer and heart disease — while killing far less. Why? Politics, pure and simple.

For all the attention paid to AIDS and all the money spent on AIDS "awareness" and education (not to mention all the free publicity it receives in the media), when are we going to see some responsibility taken by the homosexual lobby? They are the victims of their own vices, not of public indifference, as they would have us believe.

The homosexual lifestyle is seamy and grotesque. It is responsible for the spread of disease unimaginably out of proportion to homosexuals' relatively low representation in the general population. According to Stanley Montieth, M.D., author of *AIDS: the Unnecessary Epidemic*, "The tragedy is that most people in the general population do not understand what the homosexual lifestyle really involves. The young people in our schools are being indoctrinated in their sex education classes with the idea that homosexuality is simply an alternative lifestyle...100% of homosexuals engage in fellatio; 93% engage in rectal sex; 92% of homosexuals engage in something called 'rimming' (licking in and around your partner's anus); 47% in something called 'fisting' (inserting a man's fist and arm into a man's rectum); 29% in 'golden showers' (urinating on other men); 17% in 'scat' (rolling around in human feces.) In addition, male homosexuals average between 20 and 106 partners every year — averaging 300 to 500 in a lifetime. 37% engage in sadomasochism; 20% have engaged in sodomy with more than 1,000 men. Compared to heterosexuals, male homosexuals are eight times more likely than heterosexuals to acquire hepatitis, 14 times more likely to have syphilis, and *5,000 times more likely to acquire AIDS*." (Emphasis added.)

Notwithstanding the fact that a strong case against "sex

education" *in general* can easily be made, surely if they are unfortunately still mandated, then these grotesque facts and descriptions could never go near any curriculum, no matter how accurate and no matter how softened the language was to be made. But by the same token, it continues to be the ultimate in deception to instruct about the causes and transmission of AIDS while not mentioning the primary reason for its spreading.

Clearly then, the only sane alternative is to do away with this guide and leave the matter to the parents, with whom the children are most likely to receive the most profound set of moral values with sufficient warnings and instructions regarding sexual activity.

The HIV/AIDS Curriculum Guide is riddled with references to "behaviors that could put them at risk for HIV infection" without the slightest mention that it is homosexual behavior, far and above any other, that is the culprit for spreading the disease.

The Introduction states "Like fire, the virus does not care about a person's age, race or sexual orientation." This statement gives new meaning to the notion of misleading. AIDS is probably the most discriminating disease around, and it discriminates against homosexuals. Such a blatantly false assertion is on the order of stating that lung cancer does not discriminate against smokers. There are many such examples in the guide espousing the idea that AIDS is out there, affecting "everyone."

In a question and answer section, the first question, "How do people 'catch' HIV?" is answered in a contrived "scientific" manner, blaming "sexual intercourse" in general, without admitting that transmission of the virus through homosexual sex dwarfs the rare transmission through heterosexual sex. The answer is more in keeping with stylish liberal politics than medical truths.

On the same page there is the question, "If I have friends with HIV/AIDS, can I still hang out with them?" The answer given is "Yes. You cannot get HIV/AIDS from casual contact with an infected person. You can hug, touch, and kiss your friends..." While a technical reading of this answer may be true, it certainly should raise eyebrows with parents who understand that hugging and kissing could go further, and parents should be mortified that the

EDUCATION

schools will be giving their children the go-ahead to be physically close with others who are infected. If this is not a decision for the parents, what is?

The guide states that the virus is "largely preventable" but again refuses to state how. It implies that AIDS is "anyone's" disease and there is the statement, "HIV/AIDS is a health crisis that affects everyone." True, only in the sense that everyone's taxes are used to subsidize perverted behavior. It also tells us, "...infection can be transmitted regardless of age, race, or *sexual identity*." (Emphasis added) and refers to "anyone who practices risky behavior" without, of course, identifying who and what that behavior is.

The guide contains a True and False section. Question number 1 reads, "Some people say that only gay and bisexual men are likely to be infected with HIV. True or false — and why?" The answer is "False. It is true that gay and bisexual men were one of the first populations to be hit heavily by HIV in the U.S.A., though HIV has spread through heterosexual intercourse in other countries." The answer also refers to "a rising spread" among heterosexuals, non-drug users, children, adolescents, and adults alike." These lies represent the radical homosexual propaganda machine at its best — and most dangerous. Once again, the curriculum guide is being used as a tool to garner sympathy, acceptance and funding for those who refuse to take responsibility for their own behavior. In the same answer appears the tired lie that HIV affects anyone of any "sexual orientation."

The guide is guilty of a most vile untruth on when it states, "Seventy-five percent of all infected people were exposed to the virus through unprotected heterosexual sexual intercourse."

Here we go again. In reality, the Center for Disease Control reports that two-thirds of cases worldwide were caused by homosexual or bisexual males. Another seventeen percent were caused by intravenous drug users. Another eight percent were caused by homosexual drug users. Only four percent were classified as heterosexual. And even that figure is deceptively high. Of the four percent classified as "heterosexual," about half had heterosexual contact with a person with AIDS, and the rest were merely assumed to be heterosexual because the transmission occurred in countries like Haiti and Central Africa where heterosexual transmission is believed to play a major role.

The larger point is that the guide is functioning as a propaganda tool for the radical homosexual lobby. About the only true statement in this regard is where the guide states, "There is a lot of misinformation about HIV/AIDS; people need to know the facts." How true. The guide states, "Ask: 'What are some things people do that increase the risk of HIV infection?'" If ever there was a place where homosexual behavior was the obvious answer, this was it. But the guide only mentions "sexual intercourse without a condom," needles, tattooing and drug use.

Interestingly, in stating, "STDs are more common among sexually active adolescents than among sexually active people in any other age group" the guide has no problem admitting that STDs are more common to a particular *age group*, while failing to acknowledge that they are more common to a particular *lifestyle* — the homosexual one. A chart on lists on the left side "Behavior/ Situation" and on the right side "Why It's High Risk" without mentioning homosexual sex. A sillier chart on lists different behaviors on the left side. Each behavior is followed by an *x* next to either "May lead to HIV Infection" or "Cannot transmit HIV." The behavior "Being gay or lesbian" is listed as "Cannot transmit HIV." Incredible.

Teachers are instructed to "Say: 'Why is it so important that people understand that sexual activity, not sexual identity, may put a person at risk of infection?' Answer: Some people incorrectly believe that anyone who is gay or lesbian is infected with HIV. It is important to distinguish between sexual attraction or *identity* (how a person feels) and sexual *activity* (what a person does)."

In a literal sense, this is true. However, one would be required to split hairs and make distinctions to an extreme in order to arrive at such a conclusion. Assuming that a homosexual man is more likely to have HIV than a normal man is a perfectly logical assumption. It is a stretch, to say the least, to be asked to ignore the fact that a certain *identity* is conducive to a certain *behavior*.

The guide asks: "Who are some of the people who have been unfairly 'blamed' for the AIDS epidemic? Answers: Gay people, Africans, Haitians, hemophiliacs, etc." In yet another reiteration, if "gay people" have been unfairly blamed for AIDS, then Karl Marx has been unfairly blamed for communism.

In summary, the curriculum guide, with regard to the causes and transmission of the HIV virus, has acted as a propaganda tool for the radical homosexual lobby. The guide has done this through distortions, half-truths and outright factual falsehoods. To merely correct the falsehoods would be an effort in futility for three reasons: 1. The guide is too vastly riddled with these distortions from front to back. 2. Even if the truth was revealed about homosexual culpability in the transmission of HIV, and the language softened, it could never approach anything near acceptability and age-appropriateness for grades 7, 8, and 9. 3. Since the entire general concept of "sex education" is so severely flawed, it is best to leave such matters to the wisdom and moral guidance of the parents regarding their own children.

Psychological Brainwashing and Political Correctness

The HIV/AIDS Curriculum states in several places that the guide "shall stress abstinence as the most appropriate and effective premarital protection against AIDS..." However, this admonition seems to function as a deceptive political cover for a curriculum which is riddled with instructions that serve to promote anything but abstinence. The guide encourages sexual activity, not only through its explicitness and obsession with condoms, but through the psychological advocacy of certain attitudes and ideas. The guide is explicit in its desire to shape the minds and opinions of the students, rather than provide scientific and medical facts. Essentially, the guide is promoting "values" that are undoubtedly contrary to what the parents would want.

Professor Thomas Sowell has written, "...the ostensible subject of special curriculum programs — drug education, sex education, etc. — occupies a minor part of the textbooks or class time, while psychology and values are a major preoccupation. So-called 'sex education' courses and textbooks, for example, seldom involve a mere conveying of biological or medical information. Far more often the primary thrust is toward a *re-shaping of attitudes*, not only toward sex but also toward parents, toward society, and toward life."

Indeed, more indicative of what the curriculum guide is all about appears in a shocking statement in the Introduction: "Students need to know that although sexual intercourse can present risks, sexuality is a natural and healthy part of life. HIV/AIDS instruction should not create unnecessary fears about sexuality and sexual intimacy."

If there are any traces of subtlety in that statement, there are none in the following startling paragraph: "HIV/AIDS education may mean introducing certain topics much earlier than many adults would like. We may remember our own childhood years as sheltered and may prefer not to discuss such topics as drug use, sexual intercourse, and condoms in intermediate and junior high school. Yet we cannot help students protect against HIV unless we tell them how HIV is transmitted. We must fight prejudice against those affected by HIV/AIDS by explaining that 'risky behaviors' — not being a member of a particular group —can lead to HIV infection."

In other words, the pointy-headed education bureaucrats know better what attitudes to instill in the children than the parents, not to mention that when children were "sheltered," sexually transmitted diseases were not so prevalent. In addition, the guide instructs, we must "fight prejudice" (translated: accept homosexuality as normal). What in the world does this have to do with prevention? Nothing at all, but it has plenty to do with the re-shaping of values and psychological brainwashing.

At the bottom of the same page, the guide states, "... we are giving our young people the opportunity to live and love safely.." This is clearly not talk of abstinence, but of sexual promotion.

Under Guidelines for Implementation on the guide states, "Implementing an HIV/AIDS curriculum requires consideration of many viewpoints, a thorough knowledge of content, and a deep understanding of our city's diverse cultural values and beliefs." At

EDUCATION

this point, the guide is practically making no pretense to objectivity and has set out on a course of moral relativism. The only interpretation of this statement is that if there is a culture which believes that homosexuality and sexual promiscuity are acceptable, then the schools are morally required to give that point of view equal time. Once again, there are no moral absolutes. Political indoctrination is the order of the day.

More pro-homosexual sociological claptrap appears under the appropriate heading, Sensitive and Personal Issues. "Non-traditional families may include a single parent or guardian of either sex, step-parents, grandparents, half- or step-siblings, *same-gender couples*, [emphasis added] and/or other members of the extended family." In other words, "same-gender couples" are entitled to the same societal moral assent as other families. The guide also speaks of "Same-sex attraction," indicating that an "atmosphere of acceptance" is needed. We are also told, "Sexuality can be affirmed," even though the curriculum is supposedly emphasizing abstinence.

The guide's overt promotion of indoctrination continues: "It cannot be assumed that all students are heterosexual. Teachers should be sensitive to homosexual students and the isolation that they often experience. Take care to focus on behaviors (e.g., sharing of needles/syringes/works/skin-popping equipment and high-risk sexual activities) rather than on groups of people. Avoiding generalizations and stereotyping can help every other student in the classroom. HIV/AIDS education may help reduce the problems of racism and bigotry associated with this disease."

The thought police are clearly on the march.

The guide is filled with many nutty innovative suggestions, including the suggestion that people with AIDS be invited to the classroom as an "effective teaching strategy," who will "emphasize the hope as well as the challenges of living with HIV/AIDS." Invariably, such speakers would represent the liberal point of view and act as an advocate for the views expressed in the guide, including the notion that more tax dollars are needed. Moreover, what has this to do with prevention?

The guide states, "The topic of HIV/AIDS often brings up

issues of homosexuality. [Although not in this curriculum, apparently.] In accordance with the New York City Board of Education's Resolution, Statement of Policy on Multicultural Education and Promotion of Positive Intergroup Relations, remind students that all people deserve respect and to be treated fairly. Remind students that a bias against gays and lesbians is just as serious and damaging to society as a racial, ethnic, or religious bias."

This distressing pattern of political indoctrination, of equating race and ethnicity with sexual behavior, is so pervasive in the guide, that barely a page can be turned without reading more brainwashing in political correctness. The instruction to "fight bias" appears elsewhere in the guide. How does this help to fight AIDS?

Students are asked to bring in "sexuality-related newspaper and magazine articles, advertisements, and anecdotes to promote discussion of sexual choices"; to "read and write poems, articles, stories, stage or radio plays and rap songs" as a matter of reinforcement and to "identify the community's present and projected responses to AIDS." They are also told to identify ways in which those with HIV/AIDS can "overcome the stigma."

The guide asks: "What is the best way to prevent discrimination and violence against particular groups of people?" The answer given, of course, is "better education." In other words, read this curriculum guide and everything will be alright. Students are asked to report on an "incident of discrimination or violence that they believe to have been motivated by prejudice..."

Throughout the guide, a footnote appears regarding "three types of sexual intercourse: vaginal, oral, anal." The guide recommends that to grades 7 and 8, teachers should discuss these types in response to students' questions, but in grade 9 they should *initiate* such discussion. Should not the parents have the only say in whether these topics are touched on at all?

In a discussion on the unknown origin of the HIV virus, reference is made to theories tracing HIV to a particular "place, people, animal or even laboratory." For the uninitiated, the "laboratory" theory, advanced by radical conspiracy nuts, claims that Jewish doctors in secret laboratories created the AIDS virus at the behest of the U.S. Government, in order to eliminate — through genocide — black babies. That this would be mentioned so cavalierly in the guide is beyond belief.

The guide frequently delves into the amateur psychology and self-esteem business, as when it states children should, "Make a private list.. of activities and behaviors that make you feel good about yourself... or *uncomfortable*."

The activities promoted for students include word searches, haikus (three line poems), and crossword puzzles — sort of a children's guide to political correctness and sensitivity training. The Teachers' Glossary on even sees fit to define "homophobia" as "Fear and hatred of homosexuals."

In summary, the guide is a carefully erected monument to the advancement of extreme liberal ideology, a re-shaping of attitudes — brainwashing and indoctrination of children —, and the promotion of the acceptance of immoral behaviors, sexual promiscuity and every perverse form of political correctness. And it does all of this under the guise of "education." As stated previously, the guide is so completely monstrous, that it is beyond revision. All guidance on the matters contained within it should be left to the inclinations and moral bearings of the individual parents, not the schools.

Condom-Mania

As with every other aspect of "sex education," there exists an obsessive faith among liberal social engineers in the ability of latex condoms to substantially assist in the prevention of sexually transmitted diseases. Such a faith is distinguished by the institutional promotion of condoms to children in the schools through discussions, demonstrations, and encouraging their use. The case against condoms is basically three-fold. In the first place, the conventional wisdom takes a whipping in that upon the introduction of condoms into the school scene, STDs and teenage pregnancy have not gone down, but up. Once again, the specter of moral assent —approval— to sexual activity, through the promotion of condoms, has resulted in an *increase* in sexual activity. Giving out condoms encourages promiscuity.

Secondly, there is the issue of parental authority. Only in the minds of these social engineers does the education establishment know better regarding sexual instruction than the individual parents.

Thirdly, the condom failure rate is astronomical. The curriculum guide pays lip service to the fact that condoms must be "used properly," but its obsession with and faith in condoms belies any healthy skepticism. The prophylactic assault ignores the fact that condoms slip, leak and break with regularity. As a birth control device, they fail between fifteen and thirty percent of the time for all people; the figure is undoubtedly higher for teenagers. For preventing HIV/AIDS, they are profoundly less reliable. A woman is fertile for a finite period of time each month; AIDS can be contracted any time.

Nevertheless, condom-mania runs wild throughout the guide. Their mention begins in the Introduction ("correct and consistent use of a latex condom reduces the risks associated with sexual intercourse"), and are rampant through its pages.

Important note: The Commissioner's Regulations state that, "No pupil shall be required to receive instruction concerning the methods of prevention of AIDS if the parent or legal guardian of such pupil has filed with the principal of the school which the pupil attends a written request that the pupil not participate in such instruction, with an assurance that the pupil will receive such instruction at home."

Parents are strongly advised to read the entire regulation and opt-out of the relevant part of the program, especially since the "instructions" referred to include not only supplying children with condoms, but also foams, jells and creams.

One section on condoms contains such descriptive instructions that one would think condoms second only to penicillin in effectiveness in curbing disease. Mention of oil-based lubricants, lambskin and latex are supposedly educationally necessary. One explicit statement states, "Contraceptive foams, creams, or jellies that contain nonoxynol-9, a chemical that destroys sperm and certain STD-causing agents, may, when used with latex condoms, increase the condoms' effectiveness..." Among condom-mania's pearls of wisdom is "Only water-based lubricants should be used. Oil-based lubricants (such as Vaseline or baby oil) should never be used because they can destroy the latex."

Although the Condom Demonstration Instructions apply only to 9th graders in high schools (not my school district), the "one size fits all" demonstrations should be read if for no other reason than to understand the peculiar mentality of the social engineers. The guide instructs, "Buy a contraceptive foam or lubricant..."

In summary, the enthusiasm for condom instruction, use and demonstrations is further indication that the curriculum guide is morally and educationally bankrupt and should be discarded as an offense to all moral sensibilities, but perhaps more significantly, as a danger to moral and physical health.

Explicitness

Having examined the horrendous material cited in the preceding pages, there is obviously much overlap in examining the explicit language used and its inappropriateness for 7th, 8th and 9th graders. In addition to all that has been previously mentioned, the guide includes references to mouth-to-anus sex; vaginal candida; venereal warts; preseminal fluid and masturbation. Although "explicitness" has been listed as a separate category in this analysis, the entire analysis could have come under that heading.

Conclusion

"Sex education" is a proven educational failure for the precise reason that it is not educational at all. The case against it is compelling. The education establishment has shown, once again, that it is ill-equipped to handle child psychology, moral values and the spread of sexually transmitted diseases. The HIV/AIDS Curriculum Guide, Grades 7-9, as documented in this analysis, is a monstrous collection of everything that is wrong with education, everything that is wrong for society, and most importantly, everything that is wrong for children. The guide's obsession with extreme left-wing propaganda, together with the fundamental flaws of sex education, make it inappropriate to be used as an educational device. Parents are advised to familiarize themselves with the Commissioner's Regulations in order to remove their children from being instructed in those sections in which they can do so.

Unfortunately, the Commissioner's Regulations mandate HIV/AIDS instruction. At this point, time prohibits having the regulations changed, to the extent that it would be possible. Clearly, such instructions should not be mandated at all. But under the circumstances, this guide should be discarded as offensive to education, community values and moral sensibilities. Only the parents of the individual child should assume the responsibility of informing, advising and instructing on sexual matters.

7
PROFILES

PROFILES

The Man of the Millennium

No one individual has been targeted more furiously for false historical revisionism than the man celebrated this month, Christopher Columbus. He has become perhaps the most disparaged and vilified figure of the anti-Western multicultural jihad. Rather than a "discoverer" and "explorer," Columbus has become known to these America-hating dunces of the loony left as an "invader" and "pilferer." Thankfully, Columbus has survived these scurrilous attempts to demonize him. Much to their chagrin, Columbus, now more than ever, is recognized as the most important person of the past thousand years. His impact on the world has been staggering; his legacy incalculable. He is, quite simply, the Man of the Millennium.

In preparation for the Quincentennial celebration of Columbus' discovery of the New World in 1992, the National Council of Churches, a quasi-religious left-wing outfit, issued a resolution calling Columbus' arrival "the occasion for oppression, degradation and genocide..." "For the descendants of the survivors of the subsequent invasion, genocide, slavery, 'ecocide' and exploitation... a celebration is not an appropriate observance." Suzan Shown Harzo, the leader of an alliance of Indian groups, referred to pre-1492 America as "the good old days."

Well, in the pre-Columbian "good old days," cannibalism and human sacrifice were widespread, "Caribs" routinely tortured and burned their prisoners alive, and the overall backwardness and savagery of the "indigenous peoples" astounded Columbus and the Spaniards. Descendants of those natives enjoy freedoms, standards of living, and the luxuries of modernization today that they could never have hoped to experience without the arrival of the Europeans. Perhaps most importantly, was the importation of Christianity and the humanizing effect it had on the development of the New World.

Even the priest who traveled with Columbus and became the greatest champion of the Indians' rights and most vocal critic of Spanish policies, Bartolome de Las Casas, referred to Columbus as "a gentleman of great force of spirit" who was "endowed with forbearance in the hardships and adversities which were always occurring..." Christopher (which literally means "Christ-bearer") Columbus stressed his Christian convictions in everything he did and they were undoubtedly his primary motivation for sailing to the New World. Scarcely a page of his diaries fails to mention his Christian faith. But most texts about Columbus today essentially ignore or omit his own words.

Such texts, such as a Sears-Roebuck children's book entitled *The Voyage of Columbus in His Own Words* totally omits all references to God and Christianity. But a typical passage in Columbus' journal was: "I prayed to the most merciful Lord... who put into my mind, I could feel His hand upon me... to sail to the Indies."

He informed the Spanish Monarchs that he had forbidden his men from trading unfairly with the natives and they wrote to him, directing that his men treat the Indians "very well and lovingly and abstain from doing them any injury." Of course, these directives were not always followed, but many Indians voluntarily converted to Christianity as a means of escaping the barbarism that was part of native culture.

Anti-Western revisionists deride Columbus for his alleged obsession with gold. But this is very deceiving. Columbus' interest in gold went far beyond acquiring personal wealth. The costs of his enterprise were staggering: a fleet of ships, provisions, and a crew that needed to be paid in advance. These costs were only partly underwritten by private investors and the Spanish Monarchs. With Spain's treasury depleted because of war, he had to sell the voyages on the promise of wealth in the Orient. In addition, he felt compelled to make his missions profitable for the investors. Author John Eidsmoe writes, "For those ivory-tower academics who are troubled by Columbus' desire for gold, let me offer a suggestion: Try thinking of it as a 'research grant!'"

Finally, did Columbus "steal" land from the natives? This appears to be the charge with the most credibility, but closer examination reveals gaping holes in the argument. A basic principle of international law and property rights is occupation with *claim of*

PROFILES

ownership. The Indians certainly occupied the land, but did not practice real property rights as the Europeans did. Rather, they practiced a form of temporary title, where ownership consisted of *use.* When use ceased, others were free to take the land. Land ownership in the European view, therefore, was a matter of claiming permanent title. Columbus was the first to do this. In his mind, he was certainly not stealing land. Another principle of land ownership is actual, continuous and peaceful display of the functions of government over the territory. Clearly, the Indians did not do this in any modern sense.

In the Western hemisphere, there are more cities, parks, rivers and landmarks named for Columbus than any other person. Still, his most vicious detractors cannot comprehend the irony that, without him, they would not enjoy the freedom to besmirch him. Yet another unforeseen accomplishment for the Man of the Millennium.

Goldwater: The Original Extremist

Without question, Barry Goldwater's most endearing quality was his blunt honesty. In a business filled with feckless double-talking cowards, most of whom are incapable of giving a straight answer, Mr. Conservative was a hero to the Right not only for his bedrock principles but for his classic candor. Bless him.

In its front page profile the day after Goldwater's death last week, the *New York Times* referred to him as "the recklessly candid Republican presidential candidate." Indeed, that very quality may have cost Goldwater the presidency in 1964, but the political movement which he founded would grab the prize eventually because of his uncompromising steadfastness. As George Will said at the *National Review* banquet two weeks after Ronald Reagan was elected president in 1980, "It has taken 16 years to count the votes, and Goldwater has won."

With liberals dominating both the Democratic *and* Republican parties in the 1950's, Goldwater became the political standardbearer for the conservative intellectual movement that was painstakingly infiltrating the Republican Party. Rallying behind Goldwater in 1964, conservatives captured the party, pushing Nelson Rockefeller aside and anointing Goldwater the party's nominee for president against Lyndon Johnson.

Already tagged an "extremist" for his views advocating small government, the obliteration of New Deal liberalism, and fierce anti-communism, Goldwater spoke the words in his acceptance speech which he would be most closely identified with not only in 1964, but for the rest of his life. "Extremism in the defense of liberty is no vice," he said. "Moderation in the pursuit of justice is no virtue."

The Johnson campaign seized on this as further proof of Goldwater's extremism. Goldwater's campaign slogan was, "In your heart, you know he's right." The Johnson people mocked Goldwater by saying, "In your guts, you know he's nuts."

Goldwater, vindicated by history, of course, was right. Johnson, with the most destructive presidency of the 20th Century, was the one who was nuts. Goldwater, more than anyone, was living proof that today's "extremist" is tomorrow's visionary. More importantly, Goldwater's example reveals that it is more important to tell the truth than to be captive to the political niceties of the day just to win an election. This is true not only morally but pragmatically. The power of truth — eternal verities — transcends the results of any given plebiscite.

Johnson, despite crushing Goldwater with more than 60 percent of the vote, died five years after his presidency ended, a broken, defeated failure. Goldwater outlived Johnson by a quarter century, and lived to hear even *liberal Democrats* indirectly admit that he was right. Bill Clinton in his inaugural address said, "The era of big government is over." Sure, Clinton didn't really mean it, but only because of Goldwater was he forced, for political reasons, to say it. By standing on principle, Goldwater proved to be the winner by the judgment of history.

This is not an uncommon phenomenon regarding conservatives. Ronald Reagan was also sneered at, often by other Republicans, who trembled that he was too conservative, too "extreme," had too much of an itchy finger to be allowed near the nuclear button. But the power of the truth moved the nation to the right and today Reagan is considered the barometer by which Republicans are judged. And who has had more of a positive impact on American political thought: William F. Buckley, Jr., who received only 15 percent of the vote in his only run for office, or the man who defeated him, John Lindsay?

With Reagan running for re-election in 1984, rumors began to circulate that Goldwater would repeat his "extremism" statement during his speech at the Republican National Convention. Spineless Republicans fretted publicly that this would hurt the party, painting them as too extreme once again. "I don't care what they think," Goldwater said. "I'm saying it anyway." At the podium, his voice a little shaky now at the age of 75, Goldwater began the famous statement, "And let me remind you..."

Reagan then won 49 states.

From the time he wrote his landmark book, *The Conscience of a Conservative*, to his retirement days when he referred to those "oddball groups" opposing conservative jurist Robert Bork's nomination to the Supreme Court, Barry Goldwater was a national treasure. He criticized Eisenhower's "Modern Republicanism" as a "dime store New Deal." Harry Truman was "that architect of Socialism." He voted against the civil rights acts of the 1960's as unconstitutional and opposed federal aid for education and the graduated income tax. "I will not change my beliefs to win votes," he once said. "I will offer a choice, not an echo."

Indeed, the "recklessly candid" statesman said exactly what he was thinking. Today's leadership could not hold a candle to him. The conservative "extremists" of today will always remember the example of Barry Goldwater.

Meow! Katz For Congress

Amidst the salacious political tribulations occupying the national focus and the prurient behavior that has become an American obsession, Melinda Katz has gone about the painstaking business of filling one of the 435 seats in the House of Representatives.

As the incestuous blood flows in the Democratic Primary, a battle is raging to fill the place being vacated by gun-banning Representative Chuck Schumer, a politician so far to the left that he risks falling over the edge of the American ideological spectrum. Indeed, in New York, the official name of Democratic primaries is "Us Liberals." And the race to succeed Schumer will give the country exactly what it desperately needs: one more liberal in Washington.

But Melinda Katz is different. She possesses a quality that is extremely rare, the ability to make a grown man's knees shake.

In fact, Melinda is so breathtakingly cute that all her political views are rendered meaningless. She is entitled to support for the simple reason that she is the most adorable girl in creation. Melinda carries herself with grace, elegance and a smile that melts hearts. She is a dream from which one would never want to awaken.

For these reasons, the Right Wing officially endorses Melinda Katz for Congress. Just as in "Monty Python and the Holy Grail" when it was observed that only the true Messiah would deny his divinity, it is also the case that any attempt by Melinda to disavow the endorsement will only make her all the more deserving of it.

This is not to suggest that Melinda isn't smart. She certainly is, but it simply matters much less when you are capable of illuminating a room with your mere presence. When you have the sweet looks of a goddess, your platform can say the earth is flat, gun control works, and mass immigration is a cultural gift.

Artie Trasque is a gifted editorial writer with a good heart. But his endorsement of Melinda can charitably be described as droopy and long-winded. He focuses on things that are totally irrelevant — like substantive issues. "Melinda Katz has a firm grasp of the issues and has demonstrated the ability to outline her own views, not merely spout the obligatory political lines," he writes. "Her reputation as an active servant, responsive to the needs of the community, makes her a superb choice to represent us in Washington."

Huh?

One almost expects to hear violins in the background. Of course, if Artie had the slightest grasp of what really matters, he would have simply used Melinda's photo as sufficient reason to vote for her. As Seinfeld would say, chalk one up for Superficial Man.

Moreover, Melinda's candidacy has had a positive impact in areas she herself doesn't realize. For example, atheists are now believers — not because Melinda has proselytized on the campaign trail, but because it is obvious that only the hand of a Supreme being could have created such perfection in human form. Indeed, when God gave us Melinda, he was sending us the second Eve.

But Eve, in the end, sinned and was banished from Paradise. Melinda, on the other hand, is a marked improvement on God's original handiwork. She walks on water and can part the Red Sea. And Paradise is any room Melinda happens to be in.

Only the constitutional provision against monarchy prevents Melinda from taking her proper place as Queen, rather than Congresswoman. Not even Princess Diana could match Melinda's regal glamour. It is no coincidence that Melinda sings and dances when she is not legislating, as her talent is boundless and angels always unleash the world's most beautiful music.

To say that Melinda is gorgeous, stunning, vivacious and angelic is an understatement on the order of pointing out that Mark McGwire is a mildly proficient home run hitter. Indeed, the proper adjectives have not yet been invented that could adequately do justice to Melinda's shapely aura.

This Katz, like the Broadway musical, is hoping to impress enough people to take her act to the nation's capital. When Melinda gets there, Washington will automatically be transformed from the epicenter of world power to the Garden of Eden or, more likely, heaven on earth..

In fact, as the world's most perfect woman, Melinda may even bring liberalism back to respectability — not with any policy initiative, but with that adorable smile. On a scale of one to ten, Melinda is off the charts, assuredly the Katz' meow.

Bruno: Still the Living Legend

When Bruno Sammartino, perhaps the most beloved sports figure to fans born in the 1960's, spoke out against rampant steroid use in the world of professional wrestling, he did more than risk his career. In a larger sense, he was trying to salvage the game he made famous and save its young people from the scourge that has ruined so many lives. Sammartino, the greatest champion that wrestling has ever known, became an outcast to the lords of wrestling.

"The Living Legend," as Bruno is still known, represented the game of wrestling during its renaissance in the 1960's and 70's as the longtime Worldwide Wrestling Federation Champion. To wrestling's fanatical followers, he epitomized the very essence of dignity, grace, toughness and the sense that good would always triumph over evil, in a game that was uniquely a "good vs. evil" phenomenon.

The fabric of American culture has always been impacted by the world of sports and entertainment. Just as movie icons like Jimmy Stewart and John Wayne came to embody the goodness and virtue that were quintessentially American, so too did sports heroes, who became role models to fans not only for their unique skills, but for the qualities of sportsmanship and gallantry that they possessed. Where, indeed, have you gone, Joe DiMaggio?

A poll of New York sports fans in the 1970's placed Bruno Sammartino right at the top of the popularity charts with Fran Tarkenton and Joe Namath. Wrestling, so distinguished by its violence and the nonsensical ramblings of "bad guys" like Captain Lou Albano and Superstar Billy Graham, still enjoyed an almost holy aura because of Sammartino's championship reign. He became bigger than the game itself. The Sammartino record of selling out Madison Square Garden 180 times still stands. There will never be another quite like him.

Phil Mushnick is the most insightful and influential sportswriter in New York and, probably, America. For some twenty years at the *New York Post* he has written on sports media and the cultural impact of sports. He was most responsible for uncovering the steroid scandal in the WWF. Last week he said, "Bruno Sammartino is a remarkable man. He was a true champion when wrestling still had an element of goodness. People loved him for all the right reasons."

In the early 1990's, with Sammartino long retired from the ring but still announcing and earning money from wrestling, Mushnick began a series of articles exposing the use of steroids in the game. Bruno Sammartino was his most important outspoken source. Mushnick reported that young wrestlers without enough muscle mass were told by WWF bosses to "go see the doctor." The "doctor" was one George Zahorian, who was eventually convicted in federal court of distributing illegal drugs (steroids). The whirlwind of controversy escalated to the television talk shows as Mushnick also reported on wrestling's growing pedophilia scandal: a WWF official was found to be recruiting boys at foster homes and subjecting them to abuse.

"I don't like these images," Sammartino said at the time. "I don't like the culture of drugs."

According to Mushnick, "At a time when people in wrestling were protecting their own fannies, Bruno showed great integrity. He imperiled his earning power by putting principle and decency first." Bruno Sammartino continues to stand tall at a time when basketball hoodlum Latrell Sprewell assaults his coach and tries to strangle him; when baseball's Roberto Alomar spits in the face of an umpire; when hoop freak Dennis Rodman paints his hair green and kicks a cameraman; and when ex-Yankee Steve Howe is suspended seven times for snorting cocaine. Cal Ripken, Jr. and Wayne Gretzky may be the only active athletes that embody the old virtues.

When sportscaster Marv Albert was sentenced for assaulting a woman in a Virginia hotel room, Mushnick made the point that —

given the state of our cultural demise — if Albert were a star player, he would get away with it amidst a sea of sympathy. "As long as you can put money in our pocket or entertain us, all will be forgiven," he wrote.

Steroids took the life of football star Lyle Alzado. Superstar Billy Graham, one of Sammartino's great challengers, lost both his hips to steroids. Amidst all this tragedy, Bruno always understood that his role meant more than just being a champion capable of crushing body slams. It meant being someone America's fans could look up to.

In the midst of America's cultural decline, Bruno Sammartino remains a throwback to the days when sports figures were giants — when the affection he received from the fans transcended his prowess in the ring. And that affection and admiration continue to this day. Long lines of fans await him wherever he appears, remembering the joy he brought into so many lives, always the "Living Legend."

Holy Moses!

Performing his greatest miracle since he parted the Red Sea, Charlton Heston grabbed America's cultural heathens by the throat, accused them of "storming our values" and "assaulting our freedoms," and challenged patriots to "draw your sword" in the defense of mainstream America.

The legendary actor, long a hero to conservatives, has always represented — both on screen and off — what's best about America. The qualities of heroism, virtue and the God-fearing values of a long-lost time are the very essence of Chuck Heston. In recent years, as he has lamented and grown weary of his beloved country, awash in cultural and hedonistic decline, Heston's values have manifested themselves in a vigorous political activism.

Challenging the flow of an ever decadent Hollywood, Ben-Hur has climbed back into the chariot. For several years now as the national spokesman for the much-maligned National Rifle Association, Heston has defended the beleaguered Second Amendment right to bear arms with Jeffersonian eloquence. Bucking the tide of chic tinseltown liberalism, Moses has indeed come up with some new commandments.

In a speech at the 20th Anniversary celebration of the Free Congress Foundation, he said, "A cultural war is raging across our land... killing our self-confidence in who we are and what we believe. It may be a war without a bullet or bloodshed, but with just as much liberty lost: You and your country are less free."

Heston, now Vice President of the NRA, continued, "Because you choose to own guns — affirmed by no less than the Bill of Rights — you embrace a view at odds with the cultural war lords. Your pride in who you are and what you believe has been ridiculed, ransacked and plundered. If that is the outcome of cultural war and you are the victims, I can only ask the obvious question: What will become of the right itself?" Heston has also slammed the NBC movie "Long Island Incident," about the Long Island Railroad massacre, for its "deliberate and fraudulent misrepresentation" of the NRA.

But Moses' admonitions did not end with totalitarian gun control. Rather, it covered the full spectrum of the cultural sickness that has infected the United States. For the second time, he threw those stone tablets to make his point. "Rank-and-file Americans wake up every morning, increasingly bewildered and confused at why their views make them lesser citizens. The message gets through: Heaven help the God- fearing, law-abiding, Caucasian, middle-class, apparently straight — or even worse — admitted heterosexuals, male working stiff — because, not only don't you count, you are a down-right obstacle to social progress. Your voice deserves a lower decibel level, your opinion is less enlightened... That's how cultural war works. That's what happens when a generation of media, educators, entertainers, and politicians — led by a willing President — decide the America they were born into isn't good enough anymore."

Heston went on, "The Constitution was handed down to guide us by a bunch of wise old dead white guys who invented our country.

Now some flinch when I say that. Why? It's true—they were white guys. So were most of the guys that died in Lincoln's name opposing slavery in the 1860's. So why should I be ashamed of white guys? Why is 'Hispanic Pride' or 'Black Pride' a good thing, while 'White Pride' conjures shaven heads and white hoods? I'll tell you why: cultural warfare."

Beware, Heston warns, of "the fringe propaganda of the homosexual coalition, the feminists who preach that it is a divine duty for women to hate men, and blacks who raise a militant fist with one hand while they seek preference with the other."

Arrest that man for thought crimes!

Such frank discussion on the most explosive issues of our time is practically unheard of from high profile figures. Coming from an Academy Award-winning actor, however, is nothing less than astounding. Sensing the urgency of America's cultural morass and the dispossession of those who believe in the true American ideals, Chuck Heston's warning can only be categorized as a call to arms.

The Reaganite thespian, recognizing his stature as a lethal bullhorn in the war against political correctness, understands the risks of being associated with the views he expresses — notwithstanding that those views are held (albeit silently) by the overwhelming majority of Americans. Hollywood has always impacted profoundly on American culture, but in recent years cultural paganism has drowned out the virtues embodied by the likes of Charlton Heston. Going against the tide of one's contemporaries can take its toll.

Nevertheless, at the age of 74, Chuck Heston's willingness to stand tall for the truth has inspired the next generation to which he is passing the torch of freedom. America's road ahead is treacherous and uncertain. But, once again, Moses has shown that he can still lead a great people to the Promised Land.

The Liberals' Problem with Lincoln

In these politically correct times, when revisionist history has infested the textbooks of America's schools and multicultural madness is the norm, it would be instructive to observe the unique problem that liberals encounter in a close examination of the man whose birthday is celebrated this week, Abraham Lincoln. To Eurocentrists, the revisionists' Lincoln dilemma is worth examining in order to understand why they fear the truth about America's sixteenth President.

Normally, liberals would jump at the opportunity to disparage an American hero. But in the case of Lincoln, the man who "freed the slaves," liberals have too much invested in the historical perception of Lincoln as somehow the Father of Civil Rights. Therefore, to a large degree, Lincoln has been given a free pass by anti-Western academics who would otherwise have pilloried him for his true beliefs. But, more importantly, because Lincoln has such historical moral authority, the liberals fear that his real opinions on race just might be taken seriously.

"I am not, nor ever have been in favor of bringing about in any way the social or political equality of the white and black races; I am not nor ever have been in favor of making voters or jurors of Negroes, nor of qualifying them to hold office, nor intermarry with white people."

Lincoln's words, spoken in 1858 during one of his debates with Stephen Douglas, reflect views which he reiterated many times throughout his career. Although morally opposed to slavery, Lincoln never dreamed of the kind of multi-racial society that America has become. He continued, "I will say in addition to this that there is a physical difference between the black and white races which I believe will forever forbid the two races living together on terms of social and political equality."

Lincoln never imagined the races living together as equals, or living together at all for that matter. "There is a natural disgust in the minds of nearly all white people to the idea of an indiscriminate amalgamation of the white and black races," he said. "A separation of the races is the only prevention of amalgamation." Indeed, Lincoln was so thoroughly committed to the physical separation of the races, that he prepared a five-point plan for the colonization of former black slaves to territories outside the United States upon emancipation. "The enterprise is a difficult one, but where there is a will there is a way, and what colonization needs now is a hearty will."

Today's history textbooks clearly give the impression that Lincoln wanted blacks living freely and equally in the United States. But Lincoln's views on separation and colonization were so central and so critically connected to his support for emancipation, that there is strong reason to believe he would have opposed emancipation if colonization were not linked to it. Certainly, Lincoln broke historical ground when he invited the first-ever black delegation to the White House. He did not do so, however, to discuss integration and civil rights. "You and we are different races," he told them. "We have between us a broader difference than exists between any two races. This physical difference is a great disadvantage to us both, as I think your race suffers very greatly, many of them, by living among us, while ours suffers from your presence. It is better for us both, therefore, to be separated."

Finally, the multiculturalists have been less than forthcoming about Lincoln's most famous act, the Emancipation Proclamation. He did not actually "free the slaves" but declared freedom only for the slaves in those states under Confederate control — those slaves which in reality he had no power to free.

In his very next address to Congress, Lincoln stated, "I have urged colonization of the Negroes, and I shall continue. My Emancipation Proclamation was linked with this plan... I can conceive of no greater calamity than the assimilation of the Negro into our social and political life as our equal... We cannot attain this ideal union our Fathers dreamed, with millions of an alien, inferior race among us, whose assimilation is neither possible or desirable."

It can be argued, of course, that what Lincoln said then — and what he might say now — are entirely different things. But it is revealing that the very same anti-American multiculturalists who have shamefully distorted the truth in order to criminalize so many American heroes, would ignore the actual words and deeds of one of America's and history's giants. With the failure of integration; with the strife that appears wherever multi-racialism is tried; with radical ethnic and racial demands being made constantly on the American taxpayer; with the specter of ridiculous Afrocentrism; and with multiculturalism decimating the American soul, it can more accurately be argued that Lincoln's vision of the realities of a multi-racial society have turned out to be true.

Since Lincoln is so universally revered—although by different groups for different reasons — the liberals have been caught in a bind, and are terrified at the thought that many Americans may feel that Lincoln — in the words they do not want printed in school textbooks — may have been on to something.

Michael Levin's Last Laugh

Before *The Bell Curve* exploded onto the literary and cultural scene in 1994, allowing for rational discourse in the untouchable area of racial differences in intelligence, the Thought Police took Michael Levin prisoner, told him what he could and could not think, and tried to have him fired for exercising his First Amendment rights.

The Thought Police — that fascistic segment of ivory tower academics and members of the left-wing intelligentsia — tried to destroy Michael Levin, not for anything he had done, but for what he *believes*. Levin's landmark new book, *Why Race Matters* (Praeger Publishers), is the culmination of his ordeal in the surreal. A Professor of Philosophy at the City College of New York, Levin has always been known by faculty and his mostly minority students to be a scrupulously fair professor. He is a widely published writer and no student was known to say a negative word about him, notwithstanding the fact that he is a very demanding teacher.

Levin's crucible began a decade ago during the height of the Salman Rushdie affair, when the Western intellectual community's commitment to free, unfettered expression was supposedly at its peak. He authored a solicited piece for an obscure Australian journal called *Quadrant* on American education, where he expressed the view that, "If standards are going to be raised, cultural literacy reaaserted, and college education given its old depth and focus, the American polity will have to reconcile itself to an embarrassing failure rate for blacks [because] there is now quite solid evidence that... the average black is significantly less intelligent than the average white."

Thanks to *The Bell Curve* and the fact that few experts now dispute the factualness of Levin's remarks, his words today are somewhat more acceptable, at least to the extent that the main argument today is over what *causes* the white-black IQ differential, not that it exists. At the time, it actually took more than seven months for anyone at City College to discover that Levin had written the article. As copies began circulating all over CCNY, the Faculty Senate, which purports to cherish academic freedom of expression as sacred, voted to publicly censure Levin's views as "racist prejudices" by a vote of 61 to 3. (Interestingly, when the Senate was discussing what form the censure should take, they rejected the idea of a rebuttal in writing. Hmmm.)

But the Thought Police would not stop there. City College refused to stop demonstrations which were disrupting Levin's classes. They deliberately established "parallel classes" — the exact same course at the exact same time as Levin's — and sent a letter to students advising them that they could opt out of Levin's class. Finally, the President of City College set up a committee to decide if Levin's article constituted conduct unbecoming a member of the faculty, which would then be a contract violation allowing the college to fire Levin. (All this, despite the fact that no one ever claimed Levin's views had any bearing upon his ability as a teacher; that Levin had no reason to believe anyone at CCNY would even see the article; and that the essence of what Levin wrote is scientifically irrefutable.)

With this, Levin had had enough. He sued City College in federal court on First Amendment grounds and won a smashing victory, to the point where the Court ordered CCNY to disband their tyrrancial committee. During this period, Levin was making the full gamut of television talk shows and remarked after the victory, "Well, now we finally know that the First Amendment also covers criticism of blacks." William F. Buckley's *Nationl Review* defended Levin by blasting City College's standard that "the issues Levin was writing about are to be decided not by evidentiary rules but by considering which views are politically acceptable."

When *The Bell Curve* appeared several years later, Michael Levin laughed long and hard. Not only had he been vindicated in the courts, but *The Bell Curve* authors Charles Murray and Richard Herrnstein were so mainstream and well-respected that even the liberal *New Republic* ran a front page and symposium on racial differences in average intelligence. Curiously, for someone often derided as a white supremacist, Levin very inconveniently maintains that North Asians are slightly more intelligent than whites.

Today, as publishers have gotten braver, Levin's *Why Race Matters* argues that racial dogma must be discarded and racial truths adhered to if failed policies are to be corrected., "It isn't that I opened up this unpleasant topic to annoy blacks," he says, "but whites are always blamed for black failure and that's just not right." Of course, it was not enough for the Thought Police to merely disagree with Michael Levin, they had to persecute and silence him because they knew they could not refute him.

The King Has No Clothes

When the United States Senate passed the Martin Luther King holiday ten years ago, Jesse Helms stated, "If its passage in the Senate had been by secret ballot, it would not have received twenty votes." But the senators, doing what politicians spend their careers doing, cast the "safe" vote, avoiding the racist label and various other mudballs of tolerance sure to be served up by the intelligentsia dedicated to canonizing their liberal icons.

It is virtually impossible to engage in a rational, reasonable discussion on whether Martin Luther King actually *deserves* a national holiday, so blinded by emotion are its proponents. To actually debate the issue on its merits is a losing proposition for King's supporters. Besides, why let the facts get in the way of good myth.

There are two basic cases against the King holiday. First, even if we assume that all the wonderful things propagated about King by the fourth estate and the left-culture are true (probably the most irrational assumption a sane person can make), there are still scores of great Americans who are clearly more deserving. Even the Father of Our Country had to wait eighty years after his death for Congress to finally honor him. And now in 1993, Washington's birthday is more generically referred to as "President's Day."

But it is the second case against the King holiday that will cause liberals to pull their politically correct hair out. It's called the truth. Hold onto your seats.

It was William Hoar, in his article on King several years ago, who quoted Aldous Huxley in order to describe the blind worshipers of Martin Luther King. Ignorance, he said, is usually "vincible ignorance. We don't know because we don't want to know."

Is there a doctor in the house?

The most recent clay found at King's feet was discovered in 1987 when it was revealed that "Doctor" Martin Luther King is actually no doctor. It was discovered that King had extensively plagiarized huge portions of his doctoral dissertation. This revelation came to light as a result of research done by a graduate student. Naturally, this information is either ignored or explained away.

King's PhD thesis, acquired at Boston University on the subject of the German-born theologian Paul Tillich, was plagiarized to such a large degree, that not only were entire passages and paragraphs copied verbatim, but so were *entire pages*. King was indeed a careless thief. According to Theodore Pappas in *The Martin Luther King, Jr. Plagiarism Story*, King depended almost exclusively on one source -- a dissertation written by Jack Boozer, a fellow Boston University student, whose thesis on the same topic was also handed in to the same advisor at the school.

Pappas' book shows side-by-side comparisons of King's "words" with those from the copied sources. King was so blatant in his plagiarism that he even copied Boozer's mistakes (such as a wrong page number in a footnote or a transcription error.)

Boston University, which issued King his doctorate, formed a committee which determined that King plagiarized 45 percent of the first part of his dissertation and 21 percent of the second part. Incredibly, they did not view this as grounds for revocation. As Thomas Jackson points out in *American Renaissance*, "King was a dishonest scholar and got away with it -- a small-time con-man whose degree would be revoked if Boston University had any integrity." Jackson also points out that the school hypocritically "stripped a dean of his position when it was learned he had cribbed from a Wall Street Journal article for a commencement address."

King's plagiarism on his doctoral thesis is, however, only the beginning. The most famous passages from his "I Have a Dream" speech are now known to have been taken from a 1952 sermon by a black preacher named Archibald Carey. Also, his "Letter From Birmingham City Jail," his Nobel Prize Lecture and his books *Strength to Love* and *Stride Toward Freedom* are also largely plagiarized. In fact, King's papers at Crozer Theological Seminary, where he received his bachelor's degree, are filled with material which is not his own.

In a hilarious irony, King *copyrighted* much of his plagiarized material and his estate not only continues to enforce it, but actually sued *USA Today* for unauthorized use.

Since the *Wall Street Journal* finally broke the King plagiarism story in the United States (it actually first broke in the British *Sunday Telegraph*), it has, naturally, become a very annoying and inconvenient thorn in the King myth. Indeed, the national networks still treat viewers each January to nationwide scenes of King birthday celebrants swaying arm-in-arm to "We shall overcome." Even Ted Kennedy has never lived down the fact that he cheated in law school. But with King, the myth must be maintained.

That King's educational credentials are phony, completely demolishing his moral authority, partially explains his bizarre behavior and associations. Cheating on his doctorate in the 1950's was child's play compared to the facade of virtue he lived behind in the 1960's. America is prevented, however, from seeing the entire King story by a federal judge who ruled in 1977 that fourteen file cabinets full of eavesdropping data obtained by the FBI must remain sealed for a period of fifty years. Not even the Congress, which voted King the holiday, will be permitted to inspect the microphone surveillance of King's embezzling, perverted sexual escapades and communist associations. Where are all the civil libertarians wailing about the public's right to know? Oh well, until 2027 let's go with what we do know.

What is known of the contents of the files comes basically from 64,000 pages of heavily deleted documents not covered by the court order. In addition, certain government officials who were part of the Assassinations Committee investigation and some pro-King journalists were permitted to look. One author, David Garrow, wrote *The FBI and Martin Luther King Jr.*, a virulently anti-FBI diatribe, but a book which, nontheless, reveals much of what concerned the government about Martin Luther King's communist connections.

Reverend Red

President John F. Kennedy personally took King into the Rose Garden of the White House in 1963 to warn him of his closest associates. "They're communists," Kennedy told him. "You've got to get rid of them." King refused. It was for this reason that Attorney General Robert Kennedy ordered the King taps. Two years later, an FBI memo indicatedthat President Lyndon Johnson "is reluctant to expose King's communist connections because of the harm it would do to the civil-rights movement."

Stanley Levison, a member of the Executive Committee of the Communist Party, was directly involved with the illegal funding of the Communist Party, U.S.A. by the Soviet Union. He was, in fact, a Soviet agent. Levison assisted in the acquisition, disbursement and management of millions of dollars of secret funds from Moscow. After being introduced to King in 1956 by Bayard Rustin, a former member of the Young Communist League, Levison began serving King's Southern Christian Leadership Conference (SCLC). Atlanta Mayor Andrew Young said recently, "Stan Levison was one of the closest friends Martin Luther King ever had."

As the King-Levison alliance blossomed, King was repeatedly warned by the Kennedys and Assistant Attorney General Burke Marshall to dump Levison. Said Marshall, "I don't know what could be more important than having the kind of Communist that this man was claimed to be by the Bureau directly influencing Dr. King." Levison advised Martin Luther King on finances, a subject he knew well as the chief administrator of Communist Party funds. In 1977 a Department of Justice Task Force stated that Levison "prepared responses to press questions directed to Dr. King from a Los Angeles radio station regarding the Los Angeles racial riots and from the 'New York Times' regarding the Vietnam War."

The FBI's Operation SOLO taped King telling Levison, "I am a Marxist." According to William Hoar, "For his part, Stanley Levison remained under FBI surveillance long after Martin Luther King's death. And with good reason. Levison was associated with Victor Lessiovsky, top Soviet official at the U.N. As reported by the late Congressman John Ashbrook, longtime ranking member on the House Committee on Internal Security: 'Lessiovsky, until recently the personal assistant to the Secretary General of the United Nations, is one of the highest ranking KGB officers ever to serve in the United States. His relationship to Levison shows that the adviser to King remained under KGB control even after leaving the Communist party financial operation.'"

At the urging of Levison, King hired Jack O'Dell as his executive assistant. Under the pseudonym "Cornelius James,"

O'Dell had been a member of the National Committee of the Communist Party, U.S.A. Unlike Levison, whose communist affiliations were secret at the time, O'Dell had a public record of such ties. According to Senator Helms, "Despite these ties and King's knowledge of them, King promoted O'Dell within the SCLC at the behest of Levison and retained his help after twice publicly claiming to have disassociated himself from O'Dell following strong and explicit warnings from the Kennedy administration about O'Dell's Communist background and affiliations."

Any disassociation by King from communists as merely cosmetic is revealed in more than the O'Dell case. Separate FBI memos noted, "King's continued contact with Clarence Jones, who is King's conduit with communist Stanley Levison" and ""Martin Luther King, Jr. was under communist discipline." There was the Reverend James Bevel, another top King aide who told the *New York Times*, "We must move to destroy Western Civilization."

Martin Luther King himself was secretly photographed at the Highlander Folk School, a communist training school, which was allied with King's Southern Christian Leadership Conference. Seated with King was Abner Berry of the Communist *Daily Worker*. Also photographed with King was Aubrey Williams, a Communist Party member whom King regarded as "one of the noble personalities of our times."

Other communists closely allied with King were terrorists Carl and Anne Braden, who blew up a black home in a white neighborhood in the name of civil rights. Also, Communist Party member James Dombrowski, who stayed at King's home, co-signed a check to King along with a registered foreign agent of Fidel Castro. Fred Shuttlesworth, King's field director, was a onetime bootlegger and communist. King also spoke at a testimonial for Henry Winston, the vice chairman of the Communist Party, U.S.A.

Said Red

Finally, there are King's own statements. He denounced anti-communism as "irrational" and "obsessive." In a speech at New

York's Riverside Church, King compared the United States with Nazi Germany, calling America "the greatest purveyor of violence in the world today." An admirer of Ho Chi Minh, King said the American military in Vietnam "may have killed a million of them [civilians] - mostly children." Our foreign policy, according to King, was motivated by "the giant triplets of racism, materialism, and militarism."

If these are not the associations and statements of a subversive, then Josef Stalin was a civil libertarian. Even liberal John Roche of Americans for Democratic Action said, "King...has thrown in with the commies." And the liberal *Life* magazine stated King's remarks were "a demagogic slander that sounded like a script for radio Hanoi."

That any American with such a record could reasonably be called a "great man" is incredible. That the government of the United States could honor such a man is downright criminal. The King holiday is the epitome of political cowardice, a monument to spineless whores who have not the decency nor the moral statesmanship to save their country from such a disgraceful stain. Senator Helms went to court to have the FBI files released before the vote in 1983. He was denounced, of course, as a racist. So why not release the files? "We don't know because we don't want to know."

Embezzler King

Contrary to liberal opinion, some Americans would actually like to know what the cabinets are hiding without waiting thirty-four more years. According to Garrow's book, Martin Luther King was a notorious embezzler. However, we will not know to what degree until 2027. The head of domestic intelligence was certain that "King had considered funneling civil-rights funds into secret foreign bank accounts, and that King had considered soliciting money from hostile foreign governments by claiming that he would use it to advance Soviet goals in America."

An FBI memo released in 1965 stated, "King has a numbered account in his bank with a balance of over one million dollars."

King of Smut

While the tapes of King were instituted because of his subversion, they also revealed a sexually perverted and grotesque criminal side to this so-called "reverend." While Corretta and the kids were home, Martin Luther King was often involved in drunken sex orgies. So extreme was King's degenerate behavior that *entire volumes* of the FBI files were labeled "obscene." Four years ago, the late Ralph Abernathy, a close friend of King's, revealed that the night before he was assassinated, two women were screaming at King in a hotel lobby. One of the women demanded to know "where he had been." The news was greeted with the usual liberal denunciation of anything that scars their secular saint. But Abernathy's anecdote was relatively mild compared to the lurid escapades King was regularly involved in. Commenting on what they had heard on tape, an aide to President Johnson described the files as "an erotic book." LBJ himself remarked, "Goddamn it, if only you could hear what that hypocritical preacher does sexually."

There was the "two day drunken sex orgy" at the Willard Hotel involving King, SCLC colleagues and various women. "King's Mistress" was actually a dentist's wife whose brother called King a "hypocrite." And there was the ravishing of an under-age worker by the SCLC.

Noted in the files was King's relationship with a $100-a-night white woman and the Las Vegas prostitute who complained of the violence that King personally subjected her to. King was also taped at the Los Angeles Hyatt House Motel making sexually explicit remarks about Mrs. Kennedy.

A separate FBI report refers to an "intoxicated" King who threatened to "leap from the 13th floor of the hotel if the woman would not say she loved him." According to Garrow, some of those who encountered King were not "accustomed to the style in which King and his closest colleagues partied." Some civil rights insiders worried about the damage that would be done to the movement if King's "unholy trilogy of sex, Communism, and finances" were discovered. Another memo spoke of exposing King for the "clerical fraud and Marxist he is."

So now Americans, as a sacrifice to the radical "civil rights" movement, must reflect each January on a man who plagiarized his doctorate, associated with and operated under the heavy influence of communists while American boys were dying fighting them, embezzled millions of dollars to his own bank accounts, and preached the Gospel while living the life of a sexually deviant adulterer. And we are forbidden to know the whole story until 2027. As William Hoar asserted, "When the King files are opened, posterity is going to think us mad for having honored this man above every other American civilian in our history."

In the meantime, happy Martin Luther King Day.

8
BOOK REVIEWS

White, Black, a Liberal Hack

Andrew Hacker has written a book for which my bleeding heart has been aching. Actually, *Two Nations: Black and White, Separate, Hostile, Unequal* is a rather candid review on a topic which is almost never treated candidly.

Race is the most dishonestly discussed issue of our time. It is the one topic that makes grown people tremble. Hacker approaches the issue honestly even when I disagree with him and even when I think he errs badly. Discussions of race are generally so dishonest that Hacker's candor cannot help but be welcome. Displaying an obviously liberal slant, Hacker nonetheless confronts many distressing facts that America's intelligentsia will not touch.

For example, Hacker takes the position that yes, certain human characteristics and personal traits can be attributed to one's race or ethnicity — an admission that stereotypes have their basis in reality — a position liberals shudder at, and a position that is usually denied or completely avoided. But the most important point Hacker makes is also his most devastating indictment of hypocritical liberals: in spite of all the empty talk and progressive bluster, when making decisions on their own lives in the real world, all whites behave the same. Liberal whites are just as likely to move out of a neighborhood as it begins to turn black; they are just as likely to not move into a neighborhood which is black or becoming so; they are just as likely to want to send their children to safe, white, private schools. In Hacker's own words, "In spite of what we say, when it comes down to it, we're all white."

Rational Racism?

Hacker's analysis is informative when he points out the enormous disparities between the races on matters of economics, jobs, education and crime. He falls into the trap, however, of stating certain assumptions as if they are truisms beyond discussion. "Everyone agrees on the need for more black teachers..." We do?

Opining that it would be fine to have more qualified black teachers is far different than describing it as a *necessity*. Still, Hacker makes some important concessions:

"Taxicab drivers who refuse to stop for black riders base that decision on the only information they have: the race of the person raising his or her hand. Even if the driver has had some bad experiences, he understands that most black men are law-abiding citizens. At the same time he knows that some have been known to pull a gun on taxicab drivers. And that "some" is enough to make him wary about every black man... Whether a taxi driver dislikes black people is not really the issue. He may actually feel sorry for the person he left standing in the rain... Still, racism is not always based on ignorance. There can be cases where stereotyped judgments contain some elements of truth. While we can agree that taxicab drivers often make decisions on a racist basis, we might grant that in doing so they show a modicum of rationality... Sad to say, actions that are often unfair can also be reasonable, at least insofar as they are based on sufficient experience to give them a degree of validity."

It is precisely this type of sound logic that upsets liberals. Hacker also articulates the views of most Americans in the passage below. Sadly, he does not agree in the end with his own description:

"Most whites will protest that they bear neither responsibility nor blame for the conditions blacks face. Neither they nor their forebears ever owned slaves, nor can they see themselves as having held anyone back or down. Most white Americans believe that for at least the last generation blacks have been given more than a fair chance and at least equal opportunity, if not outright advantages."

Unfortunately, Hacker falls into not only his own liberalism but outright absurdity:

"As has been reiterated, there persists the belief that members of the black race represent an inferior strain of the human species... Of course, this belief is seldom voiced in public. Still, the unhappy fact remains that most white people believe that, compared with other races, persons with African ancestries are more likely to carry primitive traits in their genes. Given this premise - and prejudice - the presumption follows that most individuals of African heritage will lack the intellectual and organizational capacities the modern world requires. Most whites who call themselves conservatives hold this view, and proclaim it when they are sure of their company."

Well, I know as many conservatives this side of Clarence Thomas, and by now we have gotten used to liberals associating conservatism with racism. Such an association is implemented to further the left-wing "civil rights" agenda. Disagree with welfarism, quotas, and coddling of criminals and you are a racist. Of course, it is the modern white liberal who also harbors the belief (secretly) that blacks are inferior by implying, through welfarism and affirmative action, that blacks cannot make it on their own. This brand of liberal racism, which Roy Innis calls "reflexive" or "compensatory" racism, seeks to compensate blacks for "prior injustices" by providing benefits which liberals feel, down deep, blacks cannot attain without help.

Hacker is frustrating in that he castigates liberals for their guilt but then falls victim to it himself:

"Some people enjoy feeling guilty, indeed savor the sensation. It can also express a desire for punishment: a conscience-stricken oppressor asks to be told how he has erred, so that he may mend his ways. We have seen how this operates with white people who seek the approval of blacks, which is taken as absolving them of racism... It appears to run deeper among Jews and Congregationalists than, say, Baptists or Mormons."

The most disappointing part of *Two Nations* is Hacker's discussion of black crime. At best, he spouts the same tired liberal blather. At worst, his pronouncements border on the incredible. "Can this nation have an unstated strategy for annihilating your [black] people? How else can one explain... the incarceration of a whole generation of your men?"

Wonderful. So the reprehensible disproportion of black men committing violent crimes is attributable to some secret white plot, not to the very people who choose to rape, murder, and mug. It is white America which forces this behavior on these low-life predators. Don't liberals ever tire of this nonsense?

Liberal white guilt

Hacker participates - hook, line, and sinker - in the never-ending liberal process of searching for any possible excuse to explain away black criminal behavior. Infected with the liberal white guilt he denounces in others, Hacker will subscribe to any theory that lets blacks off the hook. No one is ever responsible for his own behavior. Everything and everyone else is to blame. "Rage" is constantly cited as an excuse for black violent crime, most recently during the Los Angeles riots. "Expressions of resistance," Hacker calls black violence. He quotes "turn 'em loose" Judge Bruce Wright explaining black crime as simply breaking "a social contract that was not of their making in the first place." Are we then to deduce that a social contract that *was* of their making would legally sanction violent behavior?

"Despite constitutional safeguards," Hacker writes, "police and prosecutors and judges still find it relatively easy to ensure that one out of every five black men will spend some part of his life behind bars." Again, no blame is placed with the criminal and his act. The judges "find it easy" because these people are black, not because they happen to commit violent crimes.

Liberals simply will not accept the fact that human beings can be inherently evil and commit heinous acts for that reason. All behavior must be explained away.

Hacker is at his best when he addresses the issue of racial lifestyles and behavior in conjunction with statistics. He states that almost all residential areas are entirely white or black. What makes integration impossible is that whites, regardless of ideology, will desert neighborhoods once the black proportion reaches between 10 and 20 percent, even if the blacks are of the same economic and social standing as the whites. Even blacks in these areas, Hacker says, want this racial ratio to remain stabilized. Do not be fooled, Hacker warns, by liberal sentiments:

"White liberals want to be liked by black people, as if having their goodwill is a seal of approval. If a few choose to live in multiracial neighborhoods and send their children to racially balanced schools, at least as many find reasons to settle in outlying towns or more insulated suburbs...Liberals stand in dread of black disfavor... Upon hearing a report of a violent crime, many liberals find themselves half-consciously hoping that the perpetrator will turn out to be white. If that proves to be the case, their response will often be a sigh of relief."

It is such promising insight as this that moves the reader to disappointment when Hacker reverts to his own liberalism.

Slavery, Africa and multiculturalism make their predictable appearances in *Two Nations.* References to slavery as contributing to the black plight today have gotten so annoying and ridiculous that only charlatans, professional victims, and guilt-ridden whites give it a serious forum. The novelist Toni Morrison informs, "At no moment in my life have I ever felt as though I were an American." No, but she has no problem making big American bucks in a country she is disparaging.

Oppressive Eurocentrism

We are told by radical black educators that minority students are "the victims of an intellectual and educational oppression due to the Euro-American monocultural perspective." The sewer they call multiculturalism could be defeated on the merits — revealing it as a parasitic intrusion of inferior non-Western cultures on American curriculum. But the multiculturalists do not stop there. Their version is a rewriting of history — making it whatever they want it to be. Cleopatra was black, Columbus a madman, George Washington a terrorist.

"American apartheid" is one of Hacker's obsessions. He absolutely refuses to acknowledge how fortunate blacks are to live in America, where they can achieve and attain more than anywhere else in the world; where they enjoy complete equality before the law and more rights and privileges than they could ever hope to see in any African nation where they could not complain of being a minority. For in the black nations of Africa, the black masses generally live in bondage, starvation and primitive lifestyles. They live under dictators and tribal chiefs with no civil rights to speak of and the figures in power are, of course, black. It is difficult for many to acknowledge that the events that brought black slaves to this continent hundreds of years ago, turned out to be a blessing for the American blacks of today.

At the expense of whites

Most Americans complain vaguely about reverse discrimination without realizing exactly how outrageous the advantages given to blacks actually are. For example, the University of Virginia has a deliberate policy of doubling its black students at the expense of white enrollment, no matter what it takes. It accepted over half of black applicants but less than a quarter of the whites, even though the blacks averaged a whopping 240 points lower on the Scholastic Aptitude Test.

Hacker's predictable conclusion comes on the final page. "So in allocating responsibility, the response should be clear. It is white America that has made being black so disconsolate an estate." It is highly regrettable that he offers such worn out, silly and patently absurd commentary. Newly arrived immigrants who are penniless and cannot speak English have fared better than blacks in America by looking inward. That Hacker fails to see this reveals a sorry blindness on his part, probably a result of liberal white guilt.

His book would have had a more profound impact had he placed the blame for the black plight squarely where it belongs. Responsibility belongs on the shoulders of those who refuse to assume personal responsibility for their own lives and actions; of those who continue to worship at the altar of welfarism and government solutions; of those who sympathize with and apologize for criminal behavior; and of those who parrot the gospel of the left-wing guilt culture. Hacker would have done well to advise them to take to heart the words of a famous Western writer. "The fault lies not in our stars, but in ourselves."

What "Mainstream" Blacks Think

It is always very dismaying to white liberals and other do-gooders when statements and feelings of blacks themselves reveal an anti-white paranoia that crosses into the realm of lunacy. When the very people liberals have painstakingly tried to placate give them a swift boot in the rear, it should become somewhat disheartening to realize that appeasing black militants only makes them angrier, uncompromising and ungrateful.

Carl Rowan has written a book which every white liberal should be forced to read, if only to wake them from their suicidal delusions. Carl Rowan is thought to be about as "mainstream" a black liberal as there is in America. He is no Farrakhan and is not even thought to be a Jesse Jackson. He is a nationally syndicated columnist based out of Washington who has won awards for journalism and is a successful television commentator. He has been ambassador to Finland and was director of the U.S. Information Agency.

Rowan's book, *The Coming Race War in America: A Wake-up Call*, is so ridiculously intense in its belief that all influential whites are scheming to oppress blacks, and so incoherent and poorly argued that Thomas Jackson says, "it reads like a skin-head parody of a black intellectual."

Rowan's basic thesis is that deep down all whites are white supremacists. Many of them will soon begin killing off blacks, with the approval of whites in positions of great influence. Blacks will retaliate and start killing whites, thus igniting a race war. And almost no one escapes Rowan's wrath and hostility.

While affirmative action finds it roots with the presidency of Lyndon Johnson, the policy actually began and expanded under Richard Nixon. Still, according to Rowan, Nixon was "a stealth bigot" who appealed to "the right-wing Caucasian soulless brothers." Ronald Reagan made white racism "fashionable" and "tolerated" in America. Because of Reagan, "every white supremacist figured that his time in America had come again and the bigots had a field day." Bill Clinton, says Rowan, is too cowardly to take on today's racists. Of course, the truth is that Clinton lacks the courage to take on Carl Rowan.

(For those with good memories, this is indeed the same Carl Rowan who made national news in 1988 when he shot an intruder with an illegal handgun. The man was taking a dip in Rowan's swimming pool in the middle of the night and Rowan confessed to keeping an illegal pistol in the house for protection — this after he had written a series of articles advocating the banning of all privately-owned firearms.)

Radio stars like Rush Limbaugh, Bob Grant, G. Gordon Liddy and even Howard Stern have successful shows and large audiences because "millions of white Americans are crazed with notions of white supremacy." These men, moreover, will have "a lot of the blood of America's race war victims on their hands and bloated bodies." Patrick Buchanan, Rowan's fellow columnist and television commentator, peddles "bigotry at great profit." That is, ironically, exactly what objective observers would say Rowan does with this book. Buchanan, says Rowan, talks like a "half-mad would-be dictator." Newt Gingrich, according to Rowan, "has a slaveowner mentality."

What possesses such a successful black man to espouse these views? Although whites invented affirmative action, Rowan is very ungrateful for the effort and now accuses whites of trying to abolish it in order to hold onto their privileges and oppress blacks. When affirmative action is eliminated, says Rowan, "armies of raging blacks... would go ballistic over effectuation of the proposed campaigns to roll back the meager gains" blacks have made. Furthermore, the federal courts have "surrendered to racist mob psychology as cravenly as any law officer ever did in the Reconstruction South."

Rowan feels that the O.J. Simpson trial produced more "belligerent racism" than any other event in half a century — not by the black jury that acquitted, but by racist whites. Happy about the not guilty verdict, Rowan states the trial did "enliven the insecurities of millions of white male psyches" because it involved a black man's relationship with a white woman.

Naturally, Rowan is very suspicious of militias, who will carry out the race war against blacks. Therefore, all Americans must be disarmed (again!) on the theory that white supremacists (all whites) simply cannot be permitted to have guns. Rowan never quite gets around to explaining how a black like himself could possible have become a millionaire and media star in such a racist country.

When all of Rowan's nonsense is finally sorted out, *The Coming Race War* actually serves a useful purpose. It provides a revealing insight into what many blacks really think of whites, as well as black attitudes about America even after decades of preferential treatment, billions of dollars in programs, and constant liberal appeasement of their demands. Rowan shows that some people are never — and never will be — satisfied.

Heard It Through the Grapevine

Black History Month is finally concluding and, once again, whites have had to grin and bear it. Several years ago one prominent black lamented, "They finally give us a month, and we get the one with only 28 days." If that reaction sounds just a bit paranoid, it actually pales in comparison with some of the more outlandish and incredible things that blacks believe whites are doing to them. Very few whites are aware of the preposterous nonsense that circulates among blacks regarding whites and the racist mischief whites are said to be constantly indulging in.

A remarkable and enlightening book on what blacks really believe about whites (including some things which are scientifically impossible) has been written by Patricia Turner, a black associate professor at the University of California at Davis. *I Heard it Through the Grapevine: Rumor in African-American Culture* is a comprehensive study of the most common anti-white beliefs held by blacks. What is significant in what Prof. Turner reveals is that it is not merely a handful of crazy blacks who believe this zaniness, but a discernibly large percentage of mainstream blacks that do, including many well-educated and successful blacks.

Whites, rumor has it, are constantly trying to sterilize black men. According to Prof. Turner, the soda Tropical Fantasy, which is sold by the Brooklyn Bottling Company, was said to be laced with a drug that would selectively sterilize black men only. (If whites drank it, there would be no effect.) Of course there exists no odorless, colorless substance that sterilizes anyone, much less only blacks. But due to black pressure, the Food and Drug Administration conducted extensive tests on Tropical Fantasy and, naturally, found nothing. Blacks, who Prof. Turner refers to as "the folk," would not believe the results, and attacked delivery trucks and storekeepers who stocked Tropical Fantasy, causing serious losses for Brooklyn Bottling.

Church's Fried Chicken was also said to have been doctored to sterilize black men. Again, the FDA conducted spectrometry tests and cleared Church's completely. Blacks then believed that the Ku Klux Klan persuaded the FDA to lie about the results.

The Troop Sport clothing company, founded in 1985, sold 95 percent of its clothes to blacks and Hispanics. In black circles, it was believed that the Troop name stood for "To Rule Over Oppressed People." The linings of shoes and jackets supposedly contained messages like, "Thank you, nigger, for making us rich." Blacks boycotted Troop and those young blacks who continued to wear Troop clothes were attacked as traitors. Troop spent hundreds of thousands of dollars fighting the rumor and even hired Gladys Knight and the Pips in its ad campaign. Troop's efforts failed and the company went bankrupt.

"The folk" also apparently believe that Kool menthol cigarettes are owned by the Klan because of the curious misspelling of the brand name.

Prof. Turner cites many well-publicized surveys which show that more than half of all blacks are either convinced or are reasonably sure that the United States government deliberately supplies illegal drugs to blacks as part of a genocidal plot. Ronald Reagan, it is said, ordered the spread of crack and guns in black neighborhoods.

The comedian Dick Gregory helped promote the popular rumor among blacks that the Center for Disease Control employed the FBI to commit the Atlanta child murders of the 1980's because an essential ingredient for the manufacture of wonder drugs could be obtained only by extracting it from the sex organs of young blacks. In addition, many of "the folk," including Bill Cosby, believe that AIDS was invented by the government in order to exterminate blacks.

Other absurdities commonly believed by blacks include: whites adopt Latin American babies to harvest their organs for transplants; the offices of Planned Parenthood are located in black neighborhoods to keep blacks from reproducing; George Bush started the Gulf War to kill off blacks in the military; the police deliberately let the Los Angeles riots get out of hand so blacks would look bad on television.

Why do blacks believe such nonsense? While she does not herself believe these ridiculous things, Prof. Turner's view is that whites are so implacably racist that blacks are somehow justified in thinking even the impossible is plausible. She thinks the rumors, although false, are "good" for blacks because they are "tools of resistance" and give blacks "a sense of power." Regrettably, this makes the book not just a study of credulity, but an exercise in it.

That so many blacks hold these beliefs demonstrates that they are so ill-disposed towards whites that they will swallow the most idiotic absurdities. More incredibly, it shows that blacks see whites as omnipotent—able to do anything they want, even the impossible. But perhaps most importantly, it is a revealing commentary on how blacks actually *see themselves* — as dolts, prepared, with little coaxing, to take drugs, shoot each other and get AIDS simply because scheming whites want them to.

About the Author

Frank Borzellieri is a graduate of St. John's University, where he attended on a scholarship. He works as a journalist and editorialist and has been published in major publications such as USA Today and Newsday. He currently publishes his own newsletter, "Verite'", and is working on his second book, "Lynched: A Conservative's Life on a New York City School Board." He is also a columnist for the Ledger-Observer newspaper chain in New York City.

Mr. Borzellieri has been an elected member of School Board 24 in Queens, New York, where he has attained national stature for his stands in defense of a Eurocentric curriculum. He is best known for his opposition to multicultural and bilingual education. Because of his often one-man crusades on these issues, Mr. Borzellieri has come to be recognized as a national figure. He has appeared on ABC's "20/20" for English as the official language and Fox Sunday Morning opposing the racial sellout by Texaco. He has also appeared on Geraldo Rivera, Leeza Gibbons Show, Vladimir Posner, Ricki Lake and many other television and radio programs as both guest and host.

Frank Borzellieri has been profiled in the New York Times, the Washington Times, Daily News, New York Post, Newsday, National Review, the Village Voice and many others.